HENRY JAMES

COMPREHENSIVE RESEARCH
AND STUDY GUIDE

BLOOM'S

MAJOR

NOVELISTS

EDITED AND WITH AN
INTRODUCTION BY HAROLD BLOOM

BLOOM'S MAJOR DRAMATISTS

Aeschylus

Anton Chekhov

Aristophanes

Berthold Brecht

Euripides

Henrik Ibsen

Ben Johnson

Christopher Marlowe

Arthur Miller

Eugene O'Neill

Shakespeare's Comedies

Shakespeare's Histories

Shakespeare's Romances

Shakespeare's Tragedies

George Bernard Shaw

Neil Simon

Sophocles

Tennessee Williams

August Wilson

BLOOM'S MAJOR NOVELISTS

Jane Austen

The Brontës

Willa Cather

Stephen Crane

Charles Dickens

Fyodor Dostoevsky

William Faulkner

F. Scott Fitzgerald

Thomas Hardy

Nathaniel Hawthorne

Ernest Hemingway

Henry James

James Joyce

D. H. Lawrence

Toni Morrison

John Steinbeck

Stendhal

Leo Tolstoy

Mark Twain

Alice Walker

Edith Wharton

Virginia Woolf

BLOOM'S MAJOR WORLD POETS

Geoffrey Chaucer

Emily Dickinson

John Donne

T. S. Eliot

Robert Frost

Langston Hughes

John Milton

Edgar Allan Poe

Shakespeare's Poems & Sonnets

Alfred, Lord Tennyson

Walt Whitman

William Wordsworth

BLOOM'S MAJOR SHORT STOR WRITERS

William Faulkner

F. Scott Fitzgerald

Ernest Hemingway

O. Henry

James Joyce

Herman Melville

Flannery O'Connor

Edgar Allan Poe

J. D. Salinger

John Steinbeck

Mark Twain

Eudora Welty

HENRY
JAMES

COMPREHENSIVE RESEARCH
AND STUDY GUIDE

BLOOM'S
MAJOR
NOVELISTS

Tulare County Library

EDITED AND WITH AN INTRODUCTION
BY HAROLD BLOOM

Printed and bound in the United States of America.

First Printing
1 3 5 7 9 8 6 4 2

Library of Congress Cataloging-in-Publication Data
applied for

ISBN 0-7910-6352-6

Chelsea House Publishers
1974 Sproul Road, Suite 400
Broomall, PA 19008-0914

The Chelsea House World Wide Web address is
http://www.chelseahouse.com

Series Editor: Matt Uhler
Contributing Editor: Grace Kim

Produced for Chelsea House Publishers by:
Robert Gerson Publisher's Services, Santa Barbara, CA

Contents

User's Guide

This volume is designed to present biographical, critical, and bibliographical information on the author's best-known or most important works. Following Harold Bloom's editor's note and introduction is a detailed biography of the author, discussing major life events and important literary accomplishments. A plot summary of each novel follows, tracing significant themes, patterns, and motifs in the work.

A selection of critical extracts, derived from previously published material from leading critics, analyzes aspects of each work. The extracts consist of statements from the author, if available, early reviews of the work, and later evaluations up to the present. A bibliography of the author's writings (including a complete list of all works written, cowritten, edited, and translated), a list of additional books and articles on the author and his or her work, and an index of themes and ideas in the author's writings conclude the volume.

Harold Bloom is Sterling Professor of the Humanities at Yale University and Henry W. and Albert A. Berg Professor of English at the New York University Graduate School. He is the author of over 20 books, including *Shelley's Mythmaking* (1959), *The Visionary Company* (1961), *Blake's Apocalypse* (1963), *Yeats* (1970), *A Map of Misreading* (1975), *Kabbalah and Criticism* (1975), *Agon: Toward a Theory of Revisionism* (1982), *The American Religion* (1992), *The Western Canon* (1994), and *Omens of Millennium: The Gnosis of Angels, Dreams, and Resurrection* (1996). *The Anxiety of Influence* (1973) sets forth Professor Bloom's provocative theory of the literary relationships between the great writers and their predecessors. His most recent books include *Shakespeare: The Invention of the Human*, a 1998 National Book Award finalist, and *How to Read and Why*, which was published in 2000.

Professor Bloom earned his Ph.D. from Yale University in 1955 and has served on the Yale faculty since then. He is a 1985 MacArthur Foundation Award recipient, served as the Charles Eliot Norton Professor of Poetry at Harvard University in 1987–88, and has received honorary degrees from the universities of Rome and Bologna. In 1999, Professor Bloom received the prestigious American Academy of Arts and Letters Gold Medal for Criticism.

Currently, Harold Bloom is the editor of numerous Chelsea House volumes of literary criticism, including the series BLOOM'S NOTES, BLOOM'S MAJOR DRAMATISTS, BLOOM'S MAJOR NOVELISTS, MAJOR LITERARY CHARACTERS, MODERN CRITICAL VIEWS, MODERN CRITICAL INTERPRETATIONS, and WOMEN WRITERS OF ENGLISH AND THEIR WORKS.

Editor's Note

My Introduction centers upon Isabel Archer of *The Portrait of a Lady* as Henry James's greatest parable of American Innocence and European Experience.

As there are twenty-nine distinguished critical views on five novels excerpted here, I will comment upon only a few I have found particularly useful.

Robert Emmet Long manifests acute insight into *Washington Square*, James's artistic coming-of-age.

F. W. Dupee and Leon Edel offer classic comments on the deeper aspects of *The Portrait of a Lady*, after which F. O. Matthiessen achieves the same classic status in regard to *The Wings of the Dove*, with Percy Lubbock matching him on *The Ambassadors*.

In *The Golden Bowl*, Austin Warren's account of the novel's symbolism is complemented brilliantly by John Bayley's excursus upon the course and progress of love in James's most elaborate masterwork.

Introduction

HAROLD BLOOM

Hester Prynne in Hawthorne's *The Scarlet Letter* permanently usurped the role of the American Eve. Henry James, in his little book on Hawthorne, allowed himself to be both condescending and evasive towards his authentic American predecessor, a pattern he repeated in writing about George Eliot. Both were too close for comfort, so much so that I risk that cliché with high deliberation. James's deprecation of *The Scarlet Letter* is notorious, and has not prevented several critics from noting the parallel between Hester's ultimate return to Boston, and Isabel's decision to go back to Osmond, her horrible choice of a husband.

Hester and Isabel are fascinating to compare, because they remain the major representations of an American woman anywhere in our imaginative literature, and yet their divergences ultimately transcend their resemblances. Hester necessarily is the grander figure, because she is the more audacious and heroic, but also her situation is more extreme and dramatic. By refusing to identify Dimmesdale as her partner in "sin," she defies Puritan Boston and its theocracy. More important, she never yields to them inwardly, and her self-affirmation is majestic. Aesthetically, she has other advantages over Isabel Archer. Though Isabel is beautiful, and inspires love, she experiences it only in a sisterly mode for Ralph Touchett and as a foster-mother for Pansy, Osmond's daughter by Madame Merle. Inadequate as Dimmesdale be, he has aroused a superb passion in Hester, whose every appearance in the novel radiates sexual power, whereas Isabel flees from Goodwood's fierce desire. And the wretched Osmond—hypocrite, pseudo-aesthete, fortune-hunter—dwindles away next to Hester's husband, the Satanic Chillingworth. If you add Hester's indubitable status as an artist in her embroidery, contrasted to Isabel's lack of all vocation or occupation, then Hawthorne's Eve far outshines James's.

And yet Isabel Archer more than sustains a comparison with her forerunner. Hawthorne, like many readers, is in love with Hester: one might even speak of his desiring her, since he has created her as the image of desire. But Hawthorne maintains a distance from her, whereas James could have said (though he would not) of his heroine what Flaubert had said of Emma Bovary: "I am Isabel Archer." Flaubert lovingly murders Emma, even as Tolstoy amorously murdered his Anna Karenina. James, preserving Isabel as he would himself, merely ruins her life, which is not his judgment, and which Isabel herself reversed as a possible judgment. She goes back to Osmond in order to proclaim her self-reliance, indeed to establish a continuity in her self-identity. It intrigues me that I do not resist Hester's return to Boston and her scarlet letter, whereas I both aesthetically approve yet humanly resent and am saddened by Isabel's return to Osmond. James has implied clearly enough that, by mutual consent, sexual relations have long since ceased for Osmond and Isabel, so that one does not regard Isabel as a sexual sacrifice. Nor does one regard either Goodwood or Warburton as worthy of Isabel: James has provided no alternative to Osmond, Ralph Touchett being frail and soon to die. The great enigma remains: however well we understand the aesthetic and spiritual inevitability of Isabel's decision, how can we accept it emotionally? Her initial choice of Osmond is appalling enough; her return violates our sense of fairness and increases our distance from her, despite our intense caring.

The Scarlet Letter is a romance, a genre it shares with Sir Walter Scott's Ivanhoe. *The Portrait of a Lady* is a Balzacian novel, in which Osmond and Madame Merle are motivated by financial considerations, which would be absurd in the realm of Hester, Dimmesdale and Chillingworth. Freedom in a novel is very different from independence in a romance. Both Hester and Isabel are Ralph Waldo Emerson's daughters, as it were, but Isabel is by far the more socialized figure. James certainly would have argued that Isabel, particularly at the book's conclusion, represents a significant advance in consciousness over Hester. Isabel has to be more advanced in worldly sophistication, but one wonders if her emphasis upon her own identity, and her insistence upon accepting the contract with life she has made, is not achieved at the cost of otherness, since the wretched Osmond scarcely is her concern, and Ralph Touchett is dead. Hester, befriending outcast women and brooding deeply upon the nature of human love, is at least as rich a consciousness.

Perhaps Isabel is closer to us not just because of history, but because Hester has a tragic grandeur. Isabel is vastly superior to most of us, in fineness of sensibility and of aspiration, and yet she is one of us, poor in judgment and unlucky where she had seemed luckiest. That may be why *The Portrait of a Lady* seems more relevant each passing day, in a society where American women of education and beauty are more free than ever before to choose, and to fall. ❀

Biography of
Henry James

Henry James was born on April 15, 1843 in Washington Square, New York, into a wealthy New England family. His father, Henry James Sr., was one of the best-known intellectuals in mid-19th-century America, whose friends included Thoreau, Emerson and Hawthorne, and his older brother, William, earned fame in his own field of pragmatic philosophy. In his early years, James studied with tutors in Geneva, London, Paris, Bologna and Bonn, acquiring languages and an awareness of Europe that few Americans could enjoy at the time. A shy and bookish young man, James devotedly read the words of Hawthorne, Balzac and Sainte-Beuve. He attended Harvard Law School for one year when he was 19, but found that his interests lay not in law but in literature.

James published his first short story, "A Tragedy of Errors," anonymously at the age of twenty-one in the New York *Continental Monthly*. In the decade that followed, he regularly contributed stories, reviews and articles to the *Nation* and *Atlantic Monthly*. The editor of the *Atlantic Monthly*, William Dean Howells, became a close friend and mentor to the young author, and between them, the era of American realism was inaugurated, such that by his mid-twenties, James was regarded as one of the most skillful writers of short stories in America. Despite his successes, however, James was relatively slow to begin a full-length novel, and his first, *Watch and Ward*, appeared in 1871 after he had completed the traditional Grand Tour of Europe. During 1875–1876, James lived in Paris, where he sought out the Russian novelist Ivan Turgenev, whose work he admired. Turgenev introduced him into Gustave Flaubert's coterie, which included Edmond de Goncourt, Emile Zola, Alphonse Daudet and Guy de Maupassant. In this circle, James confirmed his belief in the priority of the character over "story," which became his trademark literary approach despite some criticism that his writing, in focusing on the life of the mind, failed to capture the activity of life. After these years in Paris, which were both personally and professionally profitable for James, he settled permanently in England. A year before his death, he became a British subject in loyalty to his adopted country and in protest of the United States' refusal to enter the First World War. James, although friendly and even gregarious by nature, never married.

James was an extremely prolific writer. He wrote for 51 years, producing an oeuvre of 20 novels, 112 stories, 12 plays and numerous works of literary criticism. His main themes explored the conflict between the innocence of the New World and the sophistication and wisdom of the Old, which he most vividly depicted via sensitive portraits of young American heroines whose travels abroad inevitably lead to clashes of manner and ideology. The earliest of these "American girl" figures appeared in *Daisy Miller* in 1878, after which his reputation as an international literary figure was solidified and James joined the circle of the leading Victorians including Alfred Tennyson, William Gladstone, and Robert Browning. This first phase of his career was crowned with the masterpiece *The Portrait of a Lady* (1881). The next decade of James' writing took a new turn, focusing on social reformers and revolutionaries. *The Bostonians* (1886) analyzed the struggle between Southern conservative masculinity and turn-of-the-century radical feminism in the Northeast, while *The Princess Casamassima* (1886) deals with contemporary issues of anarchist violence.

James then entered into a period of literary transition, in which he tried his hand at dramatic writing. In the years between 1890 and 1895, he wrote and produced several plays that were, at best, modest successes. *Guy Domville* (1895) was actually booed off the stage, and James retreated to fiction to try to adapt his dramatic experiences to his more successful novel form. He emerged from this period with a distinctly new method of storytelling. In *The Spoils of Poynton* (1897), *What Maisie Knew* (1897), *The Turn of the Screw* (1898), *In the Cage* (1898) and *The Awkward Age* (1899), James treated the subjects of developing consciousness and the moral education of children with his newly-acquired methods of alternating "picture" and dramatic scene, and a close adherence to one particular perspective, such that the reader could gain only the information that was seen by the character at hand.

By the start of the new century, James had fully mastered his art after having spent the last decade in experimentation, and his next three novels constitute his final and "major" phase. These novels focused on a small group of characters on a relatively bare stage, which he portrayed through multiple angles of vision. Technically, his prose became dense with allusions and symbolic imagery, and James again returned to his pet fascination of the expatriated American. *The Ambassadors* (1903) was the author's personal favorite, which he regarded as his most "perfect" work. *The Wings of the Dove* (1902), in many ways, was the grander version of the earlier *The Portrait of a Lady,* as both trace the fate of an unfortunate heiress thwarted both by her innocence and others' intrigues. It was published before *The Ambassadors* although it was written after it. *The Golden Bowl* (1904) was James's final novel. A study of high-society adultery, the author divides the book in two halves—the first told by the aristocratic husband and the second by the initially unsuspecting wife.

Interspersed among his novels, plays and short stories, James wrote numerous travel essays and literary criticisms. Notable among his travel essays are *A Little Tour in France* (1885), *English Hours* (1905) and *The American Scene* (1907), which he wrote after returning to visit America after an absence of two decades. James was greatly distressed by his new vision of his native country, which had become a great industrial and political power during his long absence. The aging author expressed distaste in *The American Scene* for what he regarded as excess materialism and urban doom in American life. As a critic, James was interested in how writers consciously and unconsciously invest themselves in their written creations. He wrote on the great novelists of his century, ranging from Balzac to the Edwardian realists.

Between 1906 and 1910, James revised many of his earlier works to be collected in the New York edition of his complete works, which was published in 24 volumes. In addition to revisions, he wrote 18 significant prefaces regarding and reminiscing on his own creations. In a similar vein of nostalgia, he completed his autobiography in three separate volumes: *A Small Boy and Others* (1913), *Notes of a Son and a Brother* (1914), and *The Middle Years* (1917). James's retirement settled him in an 18th-century house at Rye in Sussex, where he died on February 28, 1916, after a prolonged illness following a stroke. Although James' public was limited during his lifetime, interest in his work was revitalized in the 1940s and 1950s, and his works were translated in many countries. In the late 20th-century, James gained a firm place in the academy as one of the most skillful novelists of literary history and a harbinger of the "stream-of-consciousness" movement. ❀

Plot Summary of
Washington Square

'At this time she seemed not only incapable of giving surprises; it was almost a question whether she could have received one—she was so quiet and irresponsive. . . . In reality, she was the softest creature in the world.'

It is not to be imagined that Doctor Sloper is the only one who is surprised to realize that his daughter is not a helpless individual. Catherine is extraordinarily unexceptional. Without any especial intelligence, beauty or charm, she resorts to using her wardrobe to try to distinguish herself, but only succeeds in making herself ridiculous to her father, who, admittedly, has never been generous in his regard of his only child. Still, even this hypercritical parent does not believe that Catherine is wholly unmarriageable; she is the heiress of ten thousand a year from her deceased mother, and stands to inherit a much larger sum from her father. However, even her valuable position as heiress does not endear her more to her father, who is ultimately more interested in protecting his savings, rather than his daughter, from falling into despicable hands.

Doctor Sloper is an extremely subtle characterization of cruelty, for his cruelty lies beneath layers of ironic but impeccable sociability. The reader has no doubt regarding Sloper's insincerity, since the author explicitly remarks that the father never addressed the daughter without irony, but the Doctor's actual disrespect for his daughter may easily be missed since he appears to take every scruple on Catherine's behalf. Frighteningly perceptive of his daughter's deep but misguided impression of the disreputable Morris Townsend, Sloper behaves as any concerned parent should. He closely inquires after the young man, discusses his visits to the house with his live-in sister, Lavinia Penniman, endeavors to make his own acquaintance with this suitor by inviting him to dine, and even pays the man's sister a visit to further collect impressions of Morris Townsend. Yet on closer inspection, it is evident that for Sloper, these are not the actions of a conscientious father, but rather those of a shrewd businessman who is loading his arsenal to defeat the man who is challenging his life's earnings.

This, for Austin Sloper, is no grim affair. Supremely confident in his own abilities, he enjoys the chase because he enjoys winning. And Sloper does not doubt a double victory—first over his daughter and next over her lover.

> The Doctor took several turns round his study, with his hands in his pockets, and a thin sparkle, possibly of irrita-tion, but partly also of something like humor, in his eye. 'By Jove,' he said to himself, 'I believe she will stick—I believe she will stick!' And this idea of Catherine 'sticking' appeared to have a comical side, and to offer a prospect of entertainment. He determined, as he said to himself, to see it out.

Even as her father delights in his cold manipulations of her most profound emotions, Catherine retains her simplicity as well as her dignity in not regarding her love for Townsend as a game to be played and won against her father. Indeed, she is 'sticking,' if that is the term preferred by Sloper, but her tenacity cannot accurately be called obstinacy in a negative sense, for Catherine 'sticks' because she loves, not because she is opposed. Her disobedience of her father, then, is merely by default, and thus absolutely passive. In assuming her love for Townsend, Catherine has no choice but to 'stick,' and no choice but to disobey.

The stakes of the 'game' are thus raised as the Doctor's amusement at his daughter's 'comical' determination gradually erodes into irrita-tion and finally anger. No longer willing to wait out her acquies-cence, Sloper proposes to Catherine that they take an extensive tour of Europe and she agrees. Father and daughter spend a year in Europe, but Catherine's pledge to Townsend does not waver. Frus-trated and furious, Sloper becomes brutal, even reckless, in his treat-ment of Catherine, and as his layers of controlled sarcasm fall away, she is forced to recognize that her most fundamental assumption that her father loves her is false. For both parties, it is a moment of high tension. With the drama of the Alps ranging behind them and with a long journey home ahead, the Doctor declares his virtual dis-inheritance of his daughter:

> 'You try my patience . . . and you ought to know what I am. I am not a very good man. Though I am very smooth externally, at bottom I am very passionate; and I assure you I can be very hard.'

Thus Catherine returns to Washington Square with a new understanding of her position and relative obligations to the two opposing loves in her life. Having felt her father's true feelings for her, she no longer desires his approval. Her emotional independence reaches to her relationship with Aunt Lavinia as well, and she regards the ridiculous woman with well-deserved resentment and disgust.

Taking matters into her own hands, Catherine announces to her lover that they must marry without her father's support, financial or otherwise. His fortune-hunting heart is stricken with the panic of loss; appropriately, the only confidante and 'guardian' that James supplies here is Mrs. Penniman, who, demonstrates an utter disregard for her niece's suffering and encourages Townsend to marry someone else who will better provide for him. Evidently, Catherine is not the only one who has undergone a shift of loyalties, and the author makes it clear that Mrs. Penniman felt no qualms at the prospect of sacrificing her niece for the sake of the dashing young man who had appealed to her infantile fancy. Morris accordingly leaves town without informing his fiancée, leaving her heart-broken and humiliated to remain in her father's house as an old maid for the rest of her life.

Yet Doctor Sloper's compulsion for control over what he considers his possessions—namely his money and Catherine—does not fade with age. On his deathbed, decades after Townsend's disappearance, he demands that his daughter promise that she will not marry him after his death. As she will not, he disowns her as he so often threatened he would. At the last, Catherine is able to see the lover of her youth once again when he returns to Washington Square some time after her father's death. In his essence and in his bank account, he is unaltered, although both Catherine and the author note that his physical beauty is considerably diminished. Mrs. Penniman is also unaltered in essence—she is responsible for his visit to her now middle-aged niece. In the scope of James's *Washington Square* it is only Catherine, who had seemed so essentially static, who ultimately undergoes personal change and maturation. ❀

List of Characters in
Washington Square

Catherine Sloper: The only daughter of an accomplished doctor. She is neither beautiful nor clever, although she does exhibit a penchant for an extravagant dress; her only wish for the first 21 years of her life is to please her father. When she falls in love with the dashing Townsend at her cousin's engagement ball, she surprises everyone with her determination in persisting against her father's opposition. Her ultimate shift in loyalty occurs when she painfully realizes that her father neither loves nor respects her. She then feels free to disobey him and marry Townsend without his blessing, only to have her heart broken a second time when the fortune-hunter shows his true colors.

Dr. Austin Sloper: A highly esteemed citizen of Washington Square, Doctor Sloper prides himself on his general competence for life. Although he is a flawless persona in the public eye, Sloper is frighteningly arrogant and dogmatically stubborn; he has no love for his only child, whom he regards as a disappointment. The Doctor opposes Catherine's marriage to Townsend, whom he accurately understands to be a fortune-hunter. He regards the conflict between himself and the lovers as a game to be won, and in his final fury at Catherine's quiet refusal to cease loving Townsend, he spitefully disowns her from his will.

Morris Townsend: A handsome but lazy and incompetent gentleman who professes love for Catherine in order to share her fortune. Catherine is unalterably impressed with his charm and social ease, but he ultimately proves that his love is false when he abandons her after realizing that her father will disinherit her if she marries him. After Doctor Sloper's death, and decades after he jilts Catherine, Townsend returns to her, still penniless and unemployed, but less handsome, in the hopes that she will marry him and provide him with even the small sum that was left to her by her mother.

Aunt Lavinia Penniman: Catherine's Aunt Lavinia, who moves into her brother's house after her sister-in-law's death, is a hopelessly ridiculous comic figure. In love with romance, she aggressively interferes in her niece's relationship with Townsend to the extent that she is more interested in feeding her own need for drama than protecting Catherine's well-being. At the last, Lavinia is a traitor to Catherine and her brother both in her antics to involve herself in the affair with Townsend.

Aunt Almond: Doctor Sloper's other sister, whom he regards with tolerable respect, unlike Lavinia. In many ways, she is the foil to her sister in that she is highly level-headed and genuinely concerned for the welfare of her niece.

Marian Almond: Catherine's cousin, whose charm and beauty are points of contrast with the older girl. She is engaged to Morris Townsend's cousin.

Mrs. Montgomery: Morris Townsend's widowed and impoverished sister, who is nonetheless forced to support her brother. When confronted by Sloper, she advises him to block Catherine's marriage to her brother. ❀

Critical Views on
Washington Square

RICHARD POIRIER ON THE COMIC SENSE

[Richard Poirier is one of the editors of *Raritan,* and of the Library of America. He is Professor of English at Rutgers University, and his books include studies of James, Mailer, and Robert Frost, as well as *A World Elsewhere* and *The Performing Self.* In this selection, Poirier highlights the attitudes of psychological experimentation and melodrama in James's characterization of Doctor Sloper.]

In terms of what has just been said, it is possible to see how *Washington Square* can be a novel in which there is great substantiality of character and extremely effective comedy without any recourse to the sort of "old civilization" referred to in James's letter. To put it briefly, *Washington Square* is in its basic situation a melodramatic fairy-tale, complete with characters who have archetypes in everyone's most rudimentary literary experience and imagination. There is no need to have read Balzac's *Eugénie Grandet* to be aware of literary analogues if we consult our memories of Cruel Father, Motherless Daughter, Handsome Lover, and Fairy God-Mother, in this case an aunt. James's transposition of these elements from the Old to the New World makes them stand out with even sharper and larger clarity. ⟨. . .⟩

We can say, in conclusion, that it is best not to think of this novel as a melodrama, but to observe that in response to the experience which it includes Dr. Sloper becomes a melodramatist and James does not. The development of his character is from scientist to melodramatist. *Washington Square* is a masterpiece if for no other reason than its making us feel the closeness of these two ways of manipulating life. The scientific attitude, with its presumptions about the predictability of a course of events, necessarily leads to melodrama when human beings refuse to imitate the logical hypotheses which are imposed upon them. Thus, *Washington Square* recapitulates the connection, noticed in every novel we have considered, between melodramatic expression and the discovery of the unpredictable.

Melodrama is the voice of the scientific mind when its theories have been defied by facts, when it is raised in a very illogical protest against the freedom of what it had assumed it had fixed. To apply this proposition to such various novels as *The American* and *Washington Square* requires only that its terms be given a legitimate latitude. In doing so it can be said that scientific logic and what is often called specifically American innocence can be almost synonymous. There is little difference between a belief in the inevitability of progress and a faith in the efficacy of scientific experiment. ⟨. . .⟩

The vocabulary of science and experimentation which is found in each of these novels places the problem of unpredictability not in Fate or in history but within the human personality and the self-delusions it contrives.

To see this is to care more for the problem of Dr. Sloper than for the chance to call him a fiend or a villain. As I pointed out at the beginning, all the circumstances of the novel are in the convention of a melodramatic fairytale. But the novel itself is a literary achievement in so far as it exceeds the expectations initially aroused by its given circumstances. Sloper is corrupted precisely because he believes in them with an accelerating desperation. In escaping from this, James is detached from the Doctor's ever-heightening ironic tone, and he leaves him at last to the ineffectual torment of his own sense of humour. Thus, in its dramatic development, *Washington Square* confirms the very nature of its own literary achievement; it shows us the melodramatic direction which was open to it but which James declined. Once again, the experience dramatized within the novel is a version of James's own artistic experience in writing it, particularly as this relates to the creation and uses of character.

—Richard Poirier, *The Comic Sense of Henry James: A Study of the Early Novels* (NY: Oxford University Press, 1960): pp. 58–72.

[Ellen Douglass Leyburn is the author of *Satiric Allegory;
Mirror of Man* and *Strange Alloy: the Relation of Comedy to
Tragedy in the Fiction of Henry James.* Leyburn explores
James's treatment of tragedy and comedy in *Washington
Square.*]

In *Washington Square* the balance is once more toward tragedy
intensified by comedy. Catherine Sloper's bringing home "her undi-
verted heart" to her faithless lover is the more moving because James
has demonstrated that "Mrs. Penniman had not made a clever
woman of her." Mrs. Penniman, with her romantic dreams of a clan-
destine marriage for the "guilty couple," after which "they would be
reconciled to her brother in an artistic tableau, in which she herself
should be somehow the central figure," is one of the chief sources of
humor in the novel; but her emptiness and incomprehension also
increase the feeling of Catherine's loneliness in the fluttering presence of her aunt. In Dr. Sloper, who "almost never addressed his
daughter save in the ironical form," James creates the chief means
both of revealing Catherine's limitations and of intensifying her suffering. And all the while the clever ironist is himself the object of
ironical satire. He can explain with perfect lucidity to Morris
Townsend's sister: "A bad husband would have remarkable facilities
for making her miserable; for she would have neither the intelligence
nor the resolution to get the better of him, and yet she would have
an exaggerated power of suffering," at the same time that he is dri-
ving her by his mockery into Morris's arms. He discovers finally that
she is "obstinate." But he never understands that he himself has
broken her heart, that "she had heart enough for that." Toward
Catherine James himself sustains a doubleness of tone in which the
surface laughter shows the tenderness: "according to her aunt's
expression, [she] went plumping down into the paternal presence.
She was really too modest for consistent pathos. . . . Poor Catherine
was conscious of her freshness; it gave her a feeling about the future
which rather added to its weight upon her mind. It seemed a proof
that she was strong and solid and dense, and would live to a great
age—longer than might be generally convenient." It is this delicate
balance of tone in the treatment of Catherine's suffering which keeps
the sensationalism of her pursuit and betrayal by the fortune

hunting Townsend from destroying the credibility of the novel. In the handling of the adventurer there is no sudden shift from satire to melodrama such as has marred the presentation of the de Belle-gardes. Morris is a preposterous figure of cardboard from his first flattering of Mrs. Penniman to his last petulant, "That was a precious plan of yours!" when he has found the middle-aged Catherine impervious to his worn-out histrionics. And the fact that he has accepted the foolish Mrs. Penniman as an accomplice has helped to make a fool of him all along. But it is the steady tone of mingled pathos and irony in James's treatment of Catherine which makes credible and moving both her having been hoodwinked by the clap-trap of Morris' pretenses and the dignity and fortitude with which she "became an admirable old maid." It persists through the very last sentence in which James consigns her to needlework after her final dismissal of Morris: "Catherine, meanwhile, in the parlor, picking up her morsel of fancy-work, had seated herself with it again—for life, as it were."

> —Ellen Douglass Leyburn, *Strange Alloy: The Relation of Comedy to Tragedy in the Fiction of Henry James* (North Carolina: University of North Carolina Press, 1968): pp. 28–30.

DANIEL J. SCHNEIDER ON THE CAGE

> [Daniel J. Schneider is the author of *The Consciousness of D. H. Lawrence: An Intellectual Biography; D.H. Lawrence, the Artist as Psychologist; The Crystal Cage: Adventures of the Imagination in the Fiction of Henry James; Symbolism: The Manichean Vision: A Study in the Art of James,* and *Conrad, Woolf & Stevens.* In this excerpt, Schneider discusses the symbolism of imprisonment and subservience in *Washington Square.*]

The symbol of the cage is prolific in James's work: it breeds a hundred symbolic associates. As James's imagination broods upon its central subject, it discovers that to put a person into the cage of the world is to fix or place him; to paralyse or petrify him; to smother him; to keep him quiet, immobile, passive. The world tolerates no freedom; it grinds out its products with an immitigable and remorseless persistence; it favors the cliché, the type, the stamped-out coin. Moreover, as we have seen, in the struggle for survival people inevitably treat others as thing—mere products or articles for use—and seek to place others in positions of immobility or passivity so as to block all threats of independent action. But James goes even further. If people may be treated as things to push or pull or handle, they may also be treated as values, quantities, treasures, or masses, and like *objets d'art* they may be collected as objects of price. Thus the imagery of petrifaction merges with that of finance and commerce, and we find James gradually working this rich vocabulary into virtually every paragraph of his novels.

He began working out these symbolic motifs even in his early fiction, where the contrast between freedom and enslavement, between "living" and the living-death of convention and propriety, is pervasively developed. Imagery of mobility and immobility is especially prominent in the early work. If Daisy Miller is all restlessness, motion, and energy, she is surrounded by a host of conventional, circumspect people who would prevent her from acting freely and spontaneously—people like the chilly Winterbourne, who is too stiff to dance, or like Winterbourne's aunt, who is "very quiet and very *comme il faut*." If Catherine Sloper responds eagerly to the theater and purchases a red-and-gold gown for a dance, "the idea of a struggle with her father, of setting up her will against his own, was heavy on her soul, and it kept her quiet, as a great physical weight keeps us motionless" (*Washington Square*). So she is condemned to genteel retirement in Washington Square, where "the ideal of quiet and of genteel refinement" prevails.

—Daniel J. Schneider, *The Crystal Cage: Adventures of the Imagination in the Fiction of Henry James* (Lawrence, Kansas: The Regents Press of Kansas, 1978): pp. 118–119.

Robert Emmet Long on Romance Shadows in the Drawing Room

[Robert Emmet Long has taught in the English departments of the State University of New York and Queens College. He is the author of *The Achieving of 'The Great Gatsby': F. Scott Fitzgerald, 1920–1925, The Great Succession: Henry James and the Legacy of Hawthorne, Henry James: The Early Novels,* and over two hundred essays and reviews. This excerpt discusses the literary influences of *Washington Square.*]

In a letter of 1880 to Howells, James called *Washington Square* "a tale purely American"; yet Buitenhuis, in the *The Grasping Imagination*, is unable to account for the novel under his classification of James's "American" writing. "The conflict," he says, "does not depend much on the national identity of the characters." Nor does James gain anything, he thinks, in setting the novel in New York City: "Since the action is practically confined to drawing-rooms, it can be divorced almost completely from local physical conditions." He concludes that lacking "formed schemata for the setting of the novel, James was forced to resort to familiar conventions in writing it . . . in this novel, if anywhere, it can be claimed that James was a kind of male Jane Austen." In his account of the novel, Buitenhuis finds himself quite unable to explain why James referred to *Washington Square* as a tale peculiarly American. An explanation is possible, but first one ought to notice how *Washington Square* came into being.

The *donnée* of the novel, furnished by James's friend, the actress Frances Kemble, is recorded in his notebook entry of February 21, 1879. Mrs. Kemble had related the story of her brother's engagement many years before to a "dull, plain, common-place girl" who stood to inherit a fortune from her father. Young Kemble was an exceptionally handsome ensign in a marching regiment; selfish and "luxurious," he was interested in the girl only for her money. The girl's father (the master of King's College, Cambridge—"the old Doctor") disapproved of the engagement and threatened to disinherit his daughter if she should marry Kemble. Convinced that the father meant to keep his word, Kemble jilted her. Later the father died, and the girl came into her inheritance. Perhaps ten years after the engagement, Kemble returned to England from knocking about in the world (still a handsome, selfish, and impecunious soldier), and once again sought to pay his addresses to her. She turned him away, even though she cared for no other man. "H. K.'s selfishness had over-reached itself and this was the retribution of time."

Mrs. Kemble's account would not, in itself, seem especially promising as the basis for a novel. What gives *Washington Square* its interest is James's superior treatment of his material. His treatment was almost certainly indebted to Balzac, as Cornelia Kelley has argued in *The Early Development of Henry James.* In "The Lesson of Balzac" (1905), James described Balzac as "the man who is really the father of us all." "I speak of him," he declares "and can only speak, as a man of his own craft, an emulous fellow-worker, who has learned from him more of the lessons of the engaging mystery of fiction than from anyone else." "The Lesson of Balzac" was written late in James's career, but he had read and admired Balzac while he was still a young man, as can be seen in his references to him in the second literary review he published. In this review of Harriet Prescott's *Azarian, An Episode* (1865), James criticized Prescott's florid style and held up Balzac's *Eugénie Grandet* to her as a model to be studied: ⟨...⟩

At the same time, *Washington Square* suggests the ambivalence of the relationship of Hawthorne and James; for if James surpasses his predecessor in realistic representation, he is also dependent on him for the archetype of psychological obsession he treats. *Washington Square* reveals the close bond between them in their shared psychological interests and in their sense of the sanctity of the individual's being. This sense of the individual's importance is part of the American democratic vision, allying James with Hawthorne despite James's allegiances to realism, and despite his criticism of democracy. With this continuation of sensibility in mind, and treatment of a common subject, it cannot be claimed that James lacked any American sources from which to draw in his conception of *Washington Square.*

—Robert Emmet Long, *The Great Succession: Henry James and the Legacy of Hawthorne* (Pittsburgh, PA: University of Pittsburgh Press, 1979): pp. 83–96.

Robert Emmet Long on Dr. Sloper and Morris Townsend as Character Doubles

[Robert Emmet Long has taught in the English departments of the State University of New York and Queens College. He is the author of *The Achieving of 'The Great Gatsby': F. Scott Fitzgerald, 1920–1925, The Great Succession: Henry James and the Legacy of Hawthorne, Henry James: The Early Novels,* and over two hundred essays and reviews. In this selection, Long analyzes Doctor Sloper and Morris Townsend as character doubles.]

The house on Washington Square dominates the action of the novel, but it is not the first house mentioned in the work that Dr. Sloper inhabits. Several years before Catherine's twenty-first birthday, he had moved uptown from a house "of red brick, with granite copings and an enormous fanlight over the door" at the older, lower end of Manhattan Island. The neighborhood had by then become "commercialized," and Dr. Sloper looked for a quieter address. "The ideal of quiet and genteel retirement, in 1835," James remarks, "was found in Washington Square, where the Doctor built himself a handsome, modern, wide-fronted house, with a big balcony before the drawing-room windows, and a flight of marble steps ascending to a portal which was also faced with white marble. This structure, and many of its neighbours, which it exactly resembled, were supposed, forty years ago, to embody the last results of architectural science." The house is clearly related to Dr. Sloper's sense of himself; it is distinctly "solid," as the doctor thinks of himself as being. Dr. Sloper knows what his "place" is in the social hierarchy of New York, and the house reflects this assumption.

To Morris Townsend, the house on Washington Square represents his own aspirations. His last name, which could be written "town's end," underscores his position as an outsider. He is without a house, living with or upon his sister, Mrs. Montgomery, who has a humble house of an indeterminate address somewhere in the dim distances of Second Avenue. Morris's attraction to the Sloper house is immediate and profound. When he dines there fairly early in the work, he reflects with satisfaction on the completeness and good taste of Dr. Sloper's wine cellar. Later, when Catherine and her father go abroad, Morris calls on Mrs. Penniman and makes himself at home in the doctor's study, smoking a leisurely cigar in the same chair in which

Dr. Sloper had smoked his. This act of usurpation is not witnessed by the doctor, but it is imagined by him while he is in Europe. Proprietor and pretender to the house, the two men are locked in conflict throughout the novel. It is in terms of the house that Morris at times regards his courtship of Catherine, as can be noticed in the scene where he returns to Washington Square with Mrs. Penniman after a discussion with her of his most advantageous next move. "His eyes," James writes, "traveled over it. . . . He thought it a devilish comfortable house."

In their will to dominate, both men regard Catherine as they might "property" that is in contention, and the antagonism between them is particularly strong because they are in many ways similar. Dr. Sloper has been a successful man, and knows it; but Morris, too, is worldly, and is alert to ways in which to advance himself. Even in their personal backgrounds, similarities can be noticed. Dr. Sloper came from modest circumstances and married an heiress. He married her, as James says, "for love," and managed a successful career that was in every way honest. One man has married an heiress, the other wishes to, and between them there is great opposition; it is as if the doctor, for all his probity, recognizes an assaultive or aggressive impulse in Morris that he understands personally only too well.

—Robert Emmet Long, *Henry James: The Early Novels* (Boston, MA: G. K. Hall & Company, 1983): pp. 90–92.

Plot Summary of
The Portrait of a Lady

> *'Do you know where you're drifting?'* Henrietta
> *pursued, holding out her bonnet delicately.*
> *'No, I haven't the least idea, and I find it very
> pleasant not to know. A swift carriage, of a dark
> night, rattling with four horses over roads that one
> can't see—that's my idea of happiness.'*

Isabel Archer's 'idea of happiness' is the momentum that pushes forward James' *Portrait*, yet Isabel's drive, unlike that of her creator, is a reckless force over which she has learned little control. Relying on her charm, her intelligence, homegrown education, and even her beauty as she would a team of horses who perhaps know the road better than she, Isabel, in many ways, is like a child who has never really been denied whatever toy or sweet she desired. She assumes that the world, or at least her world, is limitless because she has not seen its end—and even this, her own limitation, she does not know to attribute to ignorance. We must consider the author's treatment of his characters in this novel and conclude that his choice of the word *Portrait* is an extremely shrewd indication of James's understanding of his heroine, who, despite her strong spirit and sense of self, is ultimately painted by the hand and eyes of various individuals, who, each in their unique regard of the subject, render her differently. This is especially the case for Ralph Touchett, who, in his own weakness tends to regard his cousin with eyes that are perhaps too bright, for they carry a double dose of expectation—for her ambition and for his, through her, as well. And just as he imbibes her with his dreams, he provides her with his words as well.

> 'You've answered my question,' he said at last. 'You've told me what I wanted.
> I'm greatly obliged to you.'
> 'It seems to me I've told you very little.'
> 'You've told me the great thing: that the world interests you and that you want to throw yourself into it.'
> Her silvery eyes shone a moment in the dusk. 'I never said that.'
> 'I think you meant it. Don't repudiate it. It's so fine!'

> 'I don't know what you're trying to fasten upon me, for
> I'm not in the least an adventurous spirit.'

Ralph's impression of his cousin is certainly flattering, but according to Isabel herself, he is incorrect in his judgment of her. If it is actually a mistake, as she insists, it is a decisive one. The younger Touchett, who did not feel sure that he would even outlive his father, tells the old man at his deathbed that his inheritance would be better used by Isabel, that it is only this that she needs to realize her great potential. Ralph, in his illness, cannot 'throw himself into life,' as he informs Isabel she wants to, and no amount of money can help him to do that, as it can help her. Thus Ralph's faith in Isabel promptly translates into her burden of responsibility for 70,000 pounds at the execution of Mr. Touchett's will.

By the close of the first volume, Isabel has already declined to accept the proposals of the most eligible bachelors on two continents, Caspar Goodwood—who has followed her to London from the States—and Lord Warburton, whose yearly income exceeds Isabel's entire inheritance. Yet these events only serve to further whet Ralph's appetite. Fairly dancing with the impatience of seeing how she will ever top those offers, Ralph becomes daily more smug in his satisfaction of having endowed Isabel with her power to choose her destiny in full.

His complacency is completely shattered when Isabel announces her engagement to Gilbert Osmond. They quarrel, and the two cousins, who shared their lives so easily and intimately from the first day of their meeting break with one another in spirit over Isabel's marriage. Here, Ralph is completely accurate in his pronouncement:

> 'I had treated myself to a charming vision of your
> future . . . I had amused myself with planning out a high
> destiny for you. There was to be nothing of this sort in it.
> You were not to come down so easily or so soon. . . It
> hurts me,' said Ralph audaciously, 'hurts me as if I had
> fallen myself!'

As numerous critics have noted, James carefully aligned Ralph as the observer figure to Isabel the subject. But here, Ralph confesses the violation of this form, for, whether consciously or unconsciously, he has, by shifting his endowment to her, narrowed the distance between them. Significantly, this is all without her knowing, for she does not yet realize that the fortune she received was actually meant for her cousin, nor does she have any inkling that this transferal took place at all. It is perhaps the case that Isabel failed to discover the destiny that either she or Ralph envisioned because she was both ignorant and negligent of knowing the origins of herself. We know that the origin of nation was a point of great fascination for the author, as was the origin of truth. That Isabel does not carefully regard either of these areas of knowledge indicates the arrogance of youth and provincialism and it is no wonder that she is so effectively duped by Madame Merle, who, despite the appearance of her own ambiguous origins, is no such amateur. Instead, she is said to be 'armed at all points; . . . so completely equipped for the social battle."

The portrait that this personage conceives of Isabel Archer is quite a different one from that offered by Ralph. Whereas he may be overgenerous with his assessment of his cousin, Madame Merle finds that she ultimately underestimates Isabel's capacity for self-knowledge.

Ironically, Isabel's crisis for self-knowledge occurs at the point of Lord Warburton's reappearance in her life, for he comes with a renewed challenge. This time, the pressure is all covert but by no means less intense than the original proposal; for this time, the proposal is for the hand of Pansy Osmond, although she is already in love with a much less wealthy young man, Edward Rosier. Warburton's proposal is not meant to pressure Isabel, yet Osmond, greedy for the vast riches of the lordship, insists that she solidify the engagement or else be condemned as having sabotaged Pansy's future for spite. Strangely, Madame Merle also allies herself to this end, and Isabel is faced with a gap of logic that she cannot fill. And it is in this space that James drops the unlikely character of Osmond's sister, the Countess Gemini, to act the scene of revelation. And here, the Countess paints yet another portrait of Isabel Archer:

> 'My poor Isabel, you're not simple enough.'
> 'No, I'm not simple enough,' said Isabel. . . . 'What do you wish me to know?' . . .
> 'In your place I should have guessed it ages ago. Have you never really suspected?'
> 'I've guessed nothing. What should I have suspected? I don't know what you mean.'
> 'That's because you've such a beastly pure mind. I never saw a woman with such a pure mind!' cried the Countess.

Clearly, for the Countess, simplicity and pureness of mind do not coincide as the same mental element, and by evoking these two apparently similar qualities in opposition, she highlights Isabel's largely contradictory and paradoxical self. In this way, it is perhaps James's one piece of dignity given to this otherwise contemptible character that she alone has understood this complexity in the portrait of Isabel Archer.

At the last, Isabel must face the task of rendering her self-portrait. She makes bold strokes with her decision in defiance of her husband to return to Gardencourt to be with Ralph at his deathbed and their final reconciliation. Yet the self-portrait remains certainly unfinished. Although she defies Osmond to nurse her dying cousin, she will not violate the sacrament of marriage and leave him for the tenacious Goodwood. In that, the frame of her portrait is set and firm. It is James's final note of irony, then, that Madame Merle exiles herself back to her native America, while Isabel, in a grim act of self-determination, returns to Osmond and her false home. ❀

List of Characters in
The Portrait of a Lady

Isabel Archer: A 'well-born' American girl, who is brought to Europe for her 'development.' Extremely high-spirited and ambitious, Isabel values personal freedom as the most essential requirement for her happiness. As she is intelligent and beautiful, Isabel is offered several opportunities for marriages that would be considered very fortunate matches. However, she is determined to see life and the world, and thinks she will not marry. But confused by a sudden fortune and the unfamiliar social systems of Europe, Isabel falls prey to the superior sophistication of the Old World.

Ralph Touchett: Isabel's invalid cousin. He immediately falls deeply in love with her, but his felt inadequacies—his terminal illness and ugliness—disallow him to reveal his feelings. Ralph is fascinated with his cousin's spirit and ambition, and convinces his dying father to pass on his inheritance to Isabel instead. Feeling that she will now be completely free to pursue whatever course she can conceive, Ralph, in his own forced inactivity, believes he will be more than content to watch her adventures from afar. After Isabel's marriage to Osmond, for which he expressed disapproval, the relationship between the cousins is severely damaged, not to be reconciled until Isabel defies her husband in order to go to her cousin's deathbed.

Aunt Lydia Touchett: A highly individual character, she somewhat horrifies her niece with the extent of her socialization. She holds a separate residence from her husband and son, although technically, she is a devoted wife and mother. Recognizing her niece's intelligence and social potential, she brings Isabel to Europe to offer her as many 'advantages' as she can.

Uncle Touchett: Successful American banker, who has managed to keep his national flavor despite his long expatriation. He wills his son's inheritance to Isabel.

Caspar Goodwood: Wealthy New England manufacturer whom Isabel once considered marrying before she was brought to England by her Aunt. He follows her to Europe to renew his proposal, but Isabel is consistent in her answer. She regards him as a burden, as his utter masculinity is oppressive to her need for personal freedom. He is as American as Lord Warburton is British, and consequently, his repeated proposals to Isabel are heralded by Henrietta Stackpole as concomitant with her pet project of keeping Isabel from marrying a European.

Lord Warburton: British aristocrat and member of Parliament. He is said to have an astronomical 100,000 pounds a year, and his close friends regard his liberal views with an affectionate mockery. Because he is clearly an embodiment of hierarchical society, Isabel refuses his marriage proposal. He is genuinely good-natured and kind, if lacking in imagination and aesthetic subtlety.

Madame Serena Merle: Exceedingly civilized and polished in all social graces, Mme Merle makes an extremely deep impression on Isabel, who admires her even as she is mildly unsettled by the very 'unnaturalness' of the older woman's absolute perfection. Mme Merle hides a abysmal secret, which eventually involves the sacrifice of her young friend. Desiring Isabel's fortune for Pansy, the daughter she has abandoned to her father, Mme Merle executes Isabel's ultimate downfall in arranging her marriage with the heartless Osmond.

Gilbert Osmond: An American expatriate, who has lived so long in Italy that he holds no apparent national identity. He is described as a 'sterile dilettante' by Ralph Touchett, and indeed he is surrounded by an aesthetic that has failed him in that it has produced neither fame nor fortune for him. Made bitter by his personal disappointment, Osmond is a monster of cynicism and modern perversity. At Mme Merle's strong suggestion, he permits himself to be introduced to Isabel, and marries her for the conveniences of her inheritance as much as for her individual charms. Whatever love he initially felt for her evaporates in his eventual hatred of her independent mind and spirit.

Pansy Osmond: Gilbert Osmond's intensely virginal daughter, who defers to her father's every whim. She is oppressed by his refusal to acknowledge her love for Edward Rosier, but will not dare to disobey him in any capacity.

Henrietta Stackpole: American newspaperwoman and Isabel's friend. Comic in her provincialism, Henrietta makes herself ridiculous by perpetually announcing her desire to see the 'people' of

Europe, and thus undermining her own supposed purpose to do so. Henrietta adds to her querulousness as she constantly bemoans her fear that Isabel will be ruined by Europe.

Countess Gemini: Gilbert Osmond's sister, who is described as having features resembling a 'tropical bird.' She is vulgar and artificial, and has apparently deserved the notoriety that she has.

Edward Rosier: Pansy Osmond's suitor, who is not approved by her father because he is not wealthy. ❀

Critical Views on
The Portrait of a Lady

F. W. DUPEE ON THE TREE OF KNOWLEDGE

[Among F. W. Dupee's works are *Great French Short Novels,
'The King of the Cats' and Other Remarks on Writers and
Writing,* and *Henry James.* Dupee has also edited numerous
volumes including *The Question of Henry James: A Collec-
tion of Critical Essays, Selected Letters of E. E. Cummings,* and
The Selected Letters of Charles Dickens. In this selection,
Dupee describes Gilbert Osmond as an example of James's
study of the complications of modernity.]

Gilbert Osmond was James's first notable study in modern perversity. So far as his role in the plot of the *Portrait* goes, Osmond, as we
presently learn, is still the stock conspirator of melodrama, although
in the circumstances his conspiracy is not too implausible. He has
however an independent richness of being which shows, among
other things, how far James has been able to go beyond Hawthorne
in this respect. Osmond—who inevitably makes the Judge Pyn-
cheons and Chillingworths of Hawthorne look somewhat waxy—
was the reward of a searching knowledge of latter-day predicaments,
including the author's own. He is also a good instance of how James
used his international experience for wider ends. Osmond suffers
even more than Winterbourne from having lived too long in foreign
parts. A moral half-caste, he is determined to deny his American origins, while his very individuality makes it impossible for him to
become a genuine Continental. There are "no conservatives like
American conservatives," as Warburton justly remarks; and, like
those renegade Yankees in *The American* who sit happily in the
Champs Élysées and count the royal carriages, Osmond can only ape
and envy the local pomp, can only evolve for himself a caricature of
European *noblesse.* But he is very much more of a person than Tom
Tristram. In Osmond, James portrayed, ironically of course, a good
many of the possibilities of the eternal American reactionary: his
personal dandyism, his exaggerated devotion to refined pleasures,
his proud connoisseurship, his social and esthetic snobbishness
which cannot afford to temper itself with the European *noblesse
oblige,* his ancestor-worship, his rage for the static, his luxurious joy

in the possession of a general theory—pessimistic of course—of human nature. "He had an immense esteem for tradition; he had told her once that the best thing in the world was to have it, but that if one was so unfortunate as not to have it one must immediately proceed to make it." Inevitably he admires, from his connoisseur's viewpoint, the Church: "'The Catholics are very wise after all. The convent is a great institution, we can't do without it; it corresponds to an essential need in families, in society. It's a school of good manners; it's a school of repose.'" And he has had his daughter Pansy brought up by nuns, so that she shall become the perfection of the old world *jeune fille.*

To Isabel, who once rejoiced in it, Osmond's wisdom has become a torment, spoken as it is with his peculiar unction and the slow complacent shake of his small foot. "He was fond of the old, the consecrated, the transmitted; so was she, but she pretended to do what she chose with it." His conservative pose is the antithesis of the rational, the elected, thing Isabel had originally though it to be. She likes "systems," by which she means ways of life adopted and lived for high experimental purposes. It is in this that she remains so American. But Osmond's is a system in the wrong sense, or it has become that in the course of years. For he is more than a timeless satiric picture of a social-political type. His mind is shown to have had a history and to have been subject to distortion depending on circumstances. As his reactionary vehemence increases with his growing hatred of Isabel—an authentic free spirit is unendurable to him—so his marriage to her (as she, like the reader, gradually learns) was the culmination of a long development in him. He had begun, years before, by renouncing ordinary ambition in favor of a connoisseur's exquisite if modest life. In this, we are to suppose, he was originally quite genuine. But in time he has come to resent more and more his self-imposed privations; his former conviction of superiority has given way by degrees to a rank but well-concealed envy of the rich and great; until it could be said of him, as Ralph Touchett says, that "under the guise of caring only for intrinsic values Osmond lived exclusively for the world." Alas, the real free spirits are not those who make a profession of it!

—F. W. Dupee, *Henry James* (Toronto: William Sloane Associates, Inc., 1951): pp. 118–121.

[Leon Edel was a professor at New York University, and is widely considered a seminal scholar of Henry James. For the second and third volumes of his five-volume biography on Henry James, he received the 1963 Pulitzer Prize and a 1963 National Book Award. His other works include *James Joyce: The Last Journey* and *Bloomsbury: A House of Lions.* In the following article, he traces the psychological development of Isabel Archer in *The Portrait of a Lady.*]

In Isabel Archer, Henry wished to draw "the character and aspect of a particular engaging young woman," and to show her in the act of "affronting her destiny." Like her male predecessors she goes abroad a thorough provincial, with her "meagre knowledge, her inflated ideals, her confidence at once innocent and dogmatic, her temper at once exacting and indulgent." A person who is dogmatic and exacting on the strength of meagre knowledge can only be characterized as presumptuous; and there is presumption in Isabel, for all the delicacy of her feeling; presumption suggests also a strong measure of egotism. James presents her to us as a young romantic with high notions of what life will bring her; and also as one who tends to see herself in a strong dramatic light. She pays the penalty of giving "undue encouragement to the faculty of seeing without judging"; she takes things for granted on scanty evidence. The author confesses that she was "probably very liable to the sin of self-esteem; she often surveyed with complacency the field of her own nature." He speaks of her "mixture of curiosity and fastidiousness, of vivacity and indifference, her determination to see, to try, to know, her combination of the desultory flame-like spirit and the eager and personal creature of her conditions." And he adds: "She treated herself to the occasions of homage." ⟨. . .⟩

In the end one feels that Isabel's disillusionment, the damage to her self-esteem and the crushing effect of her experience, reside in the shock she receives that so large a nature should have been capable of so great a mistake; and in her realization that instead of being able to maneuver her environment, as her freedom allowed, she had been maneuvered by it. Christopher Newman had had a similar shock, in the Faubourg St. Germain. But he could write it off as the corruption and deceit of the French nobility. The deeper illusion here resides in the fact that Serena Merle and Gilbert Osmond are Americans, and the implications are that as expatriates, long divorced from their native soil, they also have been corrupted: they conceal a world of evil unknown to Isabel. America, in Henry's two novels, represented—in the larger picture—the New World's concept of its own liberties, the admixture of freedom and of power contained in America's emerging philosophy, and in the doctrines of pragmatism of which Henry's brother William was to be a founder. In drawing his novel from the hidden forces of his own experience into the palpable world of his study and observation, Henry James had touched upon certain fundamental aspects of the American character.

—Leon Edel, *Henry James: The Conquest of London 1870–1881* vol. 2, (NY: 1962): pp. 421–434.

ORA SEGAL ON *THE PORTRAIT OF A LADY*

[Ora Segal is a retired Professor of English at the Hebrew University of Jerusalem. *The Lucid Reflector: The Observers in Henry James' Fiction* is her most prominent work. This selection focuses on the role of Ralph Touchett as the observer regarding Isabel Archer.]

James, we recall, was in the habit of making the observer fall in love with the heroine for purely functional reasons: in order to deepen his sympathy and thereby give greater intensity to his narrative. However, having made the observer fall in love with the heroine, James could rarely resist the temptation of developing the potentialities of this new dramatic situation, adding to the observer's purely functional traits—curiosity, sensitivity, wit, and a lively sense of irony—the complicating elements of jealousy, resentment, vindictiveness, and exasperation. These feelings, where they occur, enrich his fictional character but may at the same time detract from his efficacy as a lucid reflector. In the case of Ralph, James does indeed make him instantly fall in love with Isabel, but no conflict between the exigencies of lucid reflection and those of convincing characterization arise. Because he is ill Ralph "loves without hope"; in fact, we are explicitly told in the introductory chapter that "the imagination of loving—as distinguished from that of being loved—had still a place in his [Ralph's] reduced sketch. He had only forbidden himself the riot of expression." In sum, since Ralph finds his spectatorship sufficiently absorbing and rewarding, his love for Isabel, though it intensifies the passionate interest he takes in her history, does not obscure his vision by detracting from his disinterestedness. If the Freers in *Lady Barbarina* are disinterested but detached, and Longmore in *Madame de Mauves* passionately concerned but lacking in objectivity, Ralph combines Longmore's intense concern with the Freers's clear-sightedness. ⟨. . .⟩

Although the authorial narrator's tone is somewhat more critical and less enthusiastic than that of the observer, he too is shown to be tenderly appreciative of the heroine's basically fine nature. His gentle irony (which plays about "poor Ralph" as well) never takes a satiric turn. In fact, in admitting to the reader that Isabel "would be an easy victim of scientific criticism if she were not intended to awaken on the reader's part an impulse more tender and more purely expectant," James dissociates his technique from the *impassibilité* advocated by Flaubert and the French naturalists, and indicates his intention of treating his heroine in a different spirit, a spirit of tender appreciation not unlike that in which Turgenev treats his heroines. In short, by analyzing Isabel's case from two viewpoints essentially similar, though varying slightly in ironic distance, James arrives at the perfect balance of criticism and sympathy, irony and admiration, severity and gentleness with which he means the reader to respond to his heroine. Moreover, by dividing the interpretive function between an authorial narrator who impresses the reader as having a full, rounded visew of Isabel's drama and an observer in whom the heroine gradually ceases to confide, and who is reduced to merely entertaining a suspicion of what her plight may be, James has combined the effect of dramatic irony—the sense that Isabel is acting out a preordained destiny—with the maximum suspense and dramatic immediacy. ⟨. . .⟩

Ralph's last words express bafflement and a weary resignation. He had perfectly understood Isabel's desire "to see life for herself," but obviously there is a certain austere, puritanical strain in his cousin's moral nature which Ralph (like many modern critics of

Henry James), who is in all other respects unreservedly intelligent, is too Europeanized to sympathize with and to respond to. What Ralph himself offers Isabel—to stay at Gardencourt, which was the seat of her first happiness—is in fact but another kind of death, a romantic escape from the consequences of her choice; and his final bafflement of course intensifies the reader's sense of Isabel's isolation—the complete solitude in which she comes to perceive the "straight path." Had the novel ended with Ralph's death, James would have achieved an effect immediately moving but false and sentimental. But Ralph's death is not the last event in the novel. Isabel's life goes on; indeed, one of James' finest strokes is his making Isabel face her most harrowing ordeal—her "battle" with Casper Goodwood—*after* Ralph's death.

The fact that James dispenses precisely at this crucial moment with the observer's interpretative commentary and does not supplement it with that of the authorial narrator is, I suggest, neither an indication of his own reservation about the moral rightness of Isabel's decision nor an attempt to mystify the reader. Rather, it is to be viewed as a strategy by means of which James emphasizes the growth of the heroine's tragic stature and her ultimate moral isolation. In his earlier short works, written in the comic-ironic key, James used to strike the authorial note in the closing as well as in the introductory passages, thus achieving a final ironic, distancing effect. In *The Portrait of a Lady,* which is written in the tragic key, James has, I have shown, employed the opposite technique—that of gradual authorial withdrawal. The interesting point is that James experimented with this technique in an early novel like *The Portrait of a Lady,* in which he uses direct authorial commentary much more extensively and freely then in the more dramatic novels of his middle and late periods.

—Ora Segal, *The Lucid Reflector: The Observer in Henry James' Fiction* (New Haven, CT: Yale University Press, 1969): pp. 37–40, 53–55.

[Peter Buitenhuis is Professor of English, Emeritus, at Simon
Fraser University. Among his many articles and books are *The
House of the Seven Gables: Severing Family and Colonial Ties*
and *The Grasping Imagination: The American Writings of
Henry James*. In this excerpt, Buitenhuis discusses James's
manipulation of perspective and self-consciousness among
the characters in *The Portrait of a Lady*.]

By this time in his career, James had quite thoroughly developed
the theory that the point of view from which the individual per-
ceived reality conditioned both what he saw and how he judged
experience. In a significant exchange with Mrs. Touchett early in
The Portrait of a Lady, Isabel asks: 'Now what is your point of view?
. . . When you criticize everything here you should have a point of
view. Yours doesn't seem to be American—you thought everything
over there so disagreeable. When I criticize, I have mine; it's thoroughly American!'

'"My dear young lady," said Mrs. Touchett, "there are as many
points of view in the world as people of sense . . . My point of view,
thank God, is personal!"' She illustrates this remark by her eccentric
behaviour throughout the novel. Each character illustrates it in his
own way. Goodwood's point of view is that of the practical, forceful
American man of business, who never can see any moral objection
to doing whatever one has the power to do to secure one's own happiness. Lord Warburton for all his 'radicalism' is stuck fast in the var-
nish of his castle and class. Even Henrietta Stackpole, that liberated
American career-woman and fifth wheel to James's novelistic coach,
is thoroughly consistent in her good-natured, ruthless desire to 'see
Europe' and in doing so missing almost every shade of the experience. Perhaps only Ralph has both the commitment to life and the
necessary detachment to transcend the limitations that perception
usually places on character. He is the only one to see the pathos and,
at the end, the promise of Isabel's situation.

Thus Henry James anticipated by some nine years the theory of
perception that his brother William was to put forward in his *Principles of Psychology* (1890): 'Whilst part of what we perceive comes

through our senses from the object before us, another part (and it may be the larger part) always comes . . . out of our own head.' James dramatizes this theory in many ways in *The Portrait*. For example, the dialogue in chapter nineteen between Madame Merle and Isabel about the relation of things to the self is essential for the definition of each character and for their respective cosmopolitan and American outlooks. 'One's self,' Madame Merle says, '—for other people— is one's expression of one's self; and one's house, one's clothes, the book one reads, the company one keeps—these things are all expressive.' Isabel replies: 'I think just the other way. I don't know whether I succeed in expressing myself, but I know that nothing else expresses me. Nothing that belongs to me is any measure of me; on the contrary, it's a limit, a barrier, and a perfectly arbitrary one.'

This brief exchange has many ramifications for the novel, and James is wise enough not to add any comment to it. Isabel has to discover, painfully, that her innocent American belief in the integrity of the self and the unimportance of what Howells had called 'the paraphernalia' are to prove woefully inadequate to her perception of the European scene, the deviousness of Osmond, and the machinations of Madame Merle herself. Emersonian self-reliance has to give way to recognition of limits, and Isabel realizes at the end of the novel that she has to return to the self that she has defined by all her previous actions and acquisitions.

—Peter Buitenhuis, *The Grasping Imagination: The American Writings of Henry James* (Toronto: University of Toronto Press, 1970): pp. 110–111.

CLAIR HUGHES ON THE COLOR OF LIFE: THE SIGNIFICANCE OF DRESS IN THE NOVEL

[Clair Hughes is an Associate Fellow at the Courtauld Institute and a Professor of English and American Literature at International Christian University in Tokyo. Her essay, *The Color of Life: The Significance of Dress in The Portrait of a Lady,* which appeared in *The Henry James*

Review, emphasizes the narrative functions of the prominent black and white color imagery in the descriptions of Isabel Archer's dress. Professor Hughes has also written a lecture entitled *Visions and Revisions of Dress in Henry James'* The Ambassadors.]

The death of Mr. Touchett in chapter 19 of *The Portrait of a Lady* closes the idyllic, garden stage of Isabel's career. She leaves white and resumes black for her uncle, but emerges from this mourning with prospects made even more brilliant, for in fairy-tale fashion she has inherited a fortune. The question of how she now sees herself, and therefore how she expresses herself to others, becomes critical. Just before Mr. Touchett's death Isabel has her famous conversation with Madame Merle on the subject of personal appearances: how the self is related to its "shell" and "cluster of appurtenances." Madame Merle believes "that a large part of myself is in the clothes I choose to wear. I've a great respect for *things.* One's self—for other people—is one's expression of one's self." Isabel, the idealist, begins reasonably enough by rejecting the notion that things can express her adequately: "Nothing that belongs to me is any measure of me. . . . Certainly the clothes which, as you say, I choose to wear, don't express me. . . . My clothes may express the dressmaker, but they don't express me. To begin with it's not my own choice that I wear them; they're imposed upon me by society." Madame Merle exposes Isabel's jejune line of reasoning by asking her if she would prefer to go without clothes, and the novel largely underwrites Madame Merle's dissent from Isabel's view. Taken to its logical conclusion, Isabel's argument would lead to a rejection of all social forms, but she does not see this. In the folk-tale, the first sign of Cinderella's translation from rags to riches was the momentous ball-gown in which she found her prince and became a princess. Isabel, too, with her American freedoms and now her American money, has become one of James's princesses, but she enters, in Dorothea Krook's words, "this infinitely encumbered and encrusted condition of life" in a black dress which effaces her identity. As this is the last description we have of her appearance until we see her three years after her marriage—again in black—the image must linger.

In the revised 1908 edition of the novel with its greater emphasis on Isabel's consciousness, James expands Isabel's impression of her first brief stay in Rome to contain "the figure of some small princess of the ages of dress overmuffled in a mantle of state and dragging a train that it took pages or historians to hold up." Tintner sees this revision as an extension of Isabel's "capacity for poetic flights to make it more credible that Osmond has caught her imagination." The change seems more specifically to prefigure Isabel's re-appearance, after marriage, in a dress whose long train weighs portentously upon her, and which James took the trouble to describe twice. Significantly Isabel's odd description of her Roman sojourn occurs only moments before Osmond's proposal of marriage. The suggestions of suffocating convention that underlie this imagined impression are to find full expression in Isabel's later physical appearance as witnessed by Ned Rosier and Ralph Touchett. Otherwise the great events in the traditional heroine's career, courtship and marriage, classic opportunities for a display of finery, pass without any notation of Isabel's appearance. Her wedding indeed disappears into a three-year gap between chapters. How then has she appeared to her "prince," Gilbert Osmond, in the crucial years between the two black dresses?

Having denied that any material object can be an expression of her self, Isabel fatally fails to take into account how the wealth she has inherited—invisible but certainly material—might define her image for others. It is the means by which she is launched into an international society. Despite her negative dress, her wealth is what Madame Merle and Osmond have seen before anything. But Osmond's aesthetic fastidiousness demands more than mere money. His ideal of womanhood, some part of which he must have seen in Isabel, is expressed in the image of his daughter, Pansy, presented to us during Osmond's courtship of Isabel as the ultimate *jeune fille*. ⟨. . .⟩

Isabel's final appearance is a disappearance, into the darkness, through the doorway which framed her original entrance across the sunlit lawns of Gardencourt—a negative of the original positive. As in that first image, she wears mourning black. The dress may seem the same but its meaning has changed: "Her attitude had a singular absence of purpose; her hands, hanging at her sides, lost themselves in the folds on her black dress." Her energetic optimism has been smothered in demoralizing grief, not only for Ralph but for herself. It takes Goodwood's kiss, an act of attempted possession, and his offer of a false notion of individual liberty, to crystallize Isabel's view of her situation and of what she needs to do: the black dress is a reinforcement of her negative answer. The measures of herself, achieved through suffering, and given material expression in her dress, sends her back through the doorway, in her own version of freedom, to Rome, Osmond and Pansy.

—Clair Hughes, "The Color of Life: The Significance of Dress in *The Portrait of a Lady*," *Henry James Review* 18, no.1 (1997): pp. 66–80.

ALEX ZWERDLING ON HENRY JAMES'S COSMOPOLITAN OPPORTUNITY

[Alex Zwerdling is Professor of English at University of California, Berkeley, focused in Modern British and American literature. His other works include *Virginia Woolf and the Real World and Orwell and the Left*. This excerpt from *Improvised Europeans: American Literary Expatriates and the Siege of London* discusses the national identities and ambiguities in the characterizations of Isabel, Madame Merle and Gilbert Osmond in *The Portrait of a Lady*.]

This self-questioning allows him to shape *The Portrait of a Lady* (1881) out of different clay. On the surface the story also records the encounter of Americans and Europeans; but although some figures like Isabel Archer's persistent suitors Lord Warburton and Caspar Goodwood are still conceived as static national stereotypes, the characters who affect her life most deeply are not. They amalgamate different national traits. Her uncle Daniel Touchett has retained his American identity despite decades of living in England. When his son Ralph complains that he has never mastered the art of English reticence, Mr. Touchett replies with easy confidence, "I say what I please." His strong sense of individuality accounts for the fact that "It had been for himself so very soluble a problem to live in England, and yet not be of it." His wife and son are similar hybrids. Though educated at Harvard and Oxford, Ralph is the product of neither country: "His outward conformity to the manners that surrounded him was none the less the mask of a mind that greatly enjoyed its independence, on which nothing long imposed itself." And Mrs. Touchett counters Isabel's innocent question about whether her point of view is American with the impatient rejoinder, "American? Never in the world; that's shockingly narrow. My point of view, thank God, is personal!"

But the least easily placed characters are Madame Merle and Gilbert Osmond, the mysterious pair who jointly trap Isabel into a disastrous marriage. They too are impossible to characterize on the basis of their origins. Isabel's attempt to classify Madame Merle only leads to confusion. She first decides she is French because she speaks the language flawlessly; but before long she speculates that "Madame Merle might be German—a German of rank, a countess, a princess." In point of fact, Madame Merle was born in the Brooklyn Navy Yard, married a Swiss businessman, lives in Italy, and is as much at home in England or France as anywhere. At the end of the novel she plans to go back—if that is the right word—to America. The impression she gives of unfathomable depths is closely tied to her cosmopolitan experience.

An even more baffling figure is her intimate friend Gilbert Osmond, and this is not merely because the two have a secret—that they were lovers when each was married, and that Pansy Osmond is their unacknowledged child. James's introduction of Osmond offers a striking contrast to his confident typecasting of Christopher Newman in *The American:* "You would have been much at a lost to determine his nationality. . . . He was one of those persons who, in the matter of race, may, as the phrase is, pass for anything." His aura of mystery deepens his interest. Ralph tells Isabel, "I don't know his antecedents, his family, his origin. For all I know, he may be a prince in disguise." It is precisely this opacity that fatally attracts Isabel: "He resembled no one she had ever seen; most of the people she knew might be divided into groups of half-a-dozen specimens. . . . Her mind contained no class which offered a natural place to Mr. Osmond—he was a specimen apart."

James's terms here offer an indirect critique of his earlier reliance on stereotypes (groups, classes, specimens) and a signal that such shortcuts are no longer helpful. All these characters (and in the long run, Isabel herself) use their expatriation as a form of freedom to construct an idiosyncratic identity independent of any given social order. What they make of this freedom is not necessarily attractive. They challenge stable expectations and institutions. They can be willful, irresponsible, devious, elusive, dangerous. They take liberties and risks, and their lives are strikingly experimental. But they are neither simple nor dull, and we want to know what they will do next.

Such characters are capable of change over time, and the capacious, slow-moving narrative is constructed to highlight this fact. The stages of Isabel's growing awareness are patiently narrated, and the notoriously inconclusive ending of the book (so frustrating for readers requiring resolution) suggests that her growth will not stop merely because the novel does. She remains a mobile character perpetually in transit. In his later preface, James notes that Isabel's consciousness, not a plot or situation, was the "single small corner-stone" of "the large building" he had constructed. The heart of his narrative lies in the maturation of her sensibility, and its most significant action is mental—the "extraordinary meditative vigil" in the middle of the book in which a solitary Isabel reflects on the decay of her marriage and the growth of her understanding in the chapter James justifiably saw as "obviously the best thing in the book."

Isabel's growth alarms her friends and relations. "O Jupiter!" exclaims her impatient brother-in-law, "I hope she isn't going to develop any more!" And her friend Henrietta Stackpole laments, "She is not the bright American girl she was. She is taking different views, and turning away from her old ideals." Even Ralph, who fosters her growth and eagerly watches from the sidelines, is not happy with the changes he observes: "The keen, free girl had become quite another person; what he saw was the fine lady who was supposed to represent something." But all these complaints hypostatize an essential, innocent Isabel whose fall into darker knowledge is regrettable. James's sense of her is different. Experience and suffering do not ennoble her but increase her understanding. They make her a competent interpreter of a world of tangled desires, of illusions and disillusionments whose complexity she can finally assess even to her own cost.

—Alex Zwerdling, *Improvised Europeans: American Literary Expatriates and the Siege of London* (NY: Basic Books, 1998): pp. 150–152.

ROBERT B. PIPPIN ON ISABEL ARCHER'S 'BEASTLY PURE MIND'

[Robert B. Pippin is Raymond W. and Martha Hilpert Gruner Distinguished Service Professor in the Committee on Social Thought, the Department of Philosophy, and the College at the University of Chicago. He is the author of several books on the modern philosophical tradition and the nature of European modernity. In *Henry James and Modern Moral Life,* Professor Pippin argues that Henry James's novels and tales engaged in a sophisticated, original exploration of moral understanding and motivation in the complex historical situation of modernity while avoiding skepticism and narrow aestheticism.]

This all means two things for the role Isabel plays in the larger moral drama of the novel. First, since she has had no guidance, no interlocutors, has been formed in the unformed culture of America, has had no help weighing and distinguishing what is important to know from what isn't, since she is so self-educated, she steps into the first scenes with a jumble of ideas, many of them clearly half-baked, none of them really attached, connected, thought through, or deep. "Forgotten things came back to her; many others, which she had lately thought of great moment, dropped out of sight. The result was kaleidoscopic. . . ." Whatever chance circumstances allowed her father to escape the hold of the only authoritative culture there was a in young America, the utilitarian and Puritan conventions that would so crush characters like Waymarsh and would produce Goodwood and Henrietta, also managed to free his brightest daughter from the same fate and to create enough suspicion and dissatisfaction and strength of will to make possible all this longing, reflection, reading and theorizing, but all in a haphazard, context-less way.

Since the question of how Isabel changes is so important, and since James is introducing her and that theme with such an emphasis on her radical rather than conventional America background (self-taught, self-reliant, brave, longing for some cultural redemption, some dimension higher than the Albany aspirations of her sisters), it is important to emphasize how much attention James draws to the consequences of her catch-as-catch-can program of self-education. James has created such a likeable character, that we might not notice that she is at first, a brash, know-it-all, somewhat self-important twenty-three-year-old, pronouncing on this or that with great confidence and authority, but who knows, finally, very little and, more dangerously, does not know what she does not know. Even our narrator, in an odd twist, "likes" her so much he hesitates to point this out! ⟨. . .⟩

Her opinions can have a "slender value"; she often only "seems to feel and think"; she wants mostly not to "appear narrow-minded," she is capable of such fatuous remarks as "Oh, I do hope they'll make a revolution!" . . . "I should delight in seeing a revolution"; and we are told that "the love of knowledge coexisted in her mind with the finest capacity for ignorance." Clearly something of both her desire for someone like Osmond, her need for such aesthetic, high-minded appearances (or even for someone who does finally seem to "speak from authority,") as well as her inability to understand what he really stands for, will have had something to do with the culture-less context within which such American "ideas" were formed.

Even more important, though, and even more American is the general shape of her most important idea, the idea that makes her at once so admirable to modern readers and that will lead her straight to her doom. What is most important to her and what others notice first about her is "independence" and her great views about independence. For that is how she understands that paradigmatic modern ideal, freedom. (The importance of this issue is signaled by the telegram the Touchetts first receive, where Mrs. Touchett describes Isabel and her sister as "quite independent," a comment that raises the question (for them and for us) of what that means: "'In a moral or financial sense? . . . that they wish to be under no obligations? Or does it simply mean that they are fond of their own way?'") This ideal is often presented with an air of paradox by James, and that is certainly appropriate since somehow the consequence of Isabel's aspiration for a "free exploration of life" will be her stepping freely into the gilded cage of Gilbert Osmond's villa and life. It is the paradox or problem at the heart of the moral issues of independence and dependence, or freedom and convention, on which so much in the novel hangs.

—Robert B. Pippin, *Henry James and Modern Moral Life* (Cambridge, UK: Cambridge University Press, 2000): pp. 130–132.

Plot Summary of
The Wings of the Dove

It is a strange narrative gesture on James's part that *The Wings of the Dove* begins with Kate Croy's unhappy interview with her father in his unflattering rooms, for after this moment, the author does not allow us to see Kate as anything but almost inhumanly competent at the business of living. In fact, it is easy to forget that Kate initially offered herself to her father, to live with him in his poverty and ill-repute; in all but these opening pages, she makes herself one with her ambitions to gain both love and fortune in spite of all odds. It is as if, after she is rejected by Lionel Croy and forced to return to her Aunt Maud, she has resolved to never again have her will be obstructed, even by this most formidable woman.

Kate's methods of expressing her will are as extraordinary as she and her purposes are. Always efficient, always effective, even in her most profound emotions, she behaves more like an awesome system rather than a human being. Her measures of patience and control are nothing if not remarkable, especially in light of her characteristic conciseness of speech, which condenses even the most convoluted dilemmas into the shortest possible route of resolution and which contains volumes of subtleties for each word uttered. It is no wonder, then, that her lover allows himself to be moved within her system, for even had he not been so prodigiously in love, he cannot help but be manipulated by Kate for Merton Densher's talents must wither in the face of such absolute pragmatism. But for all his apparent submission to Kate, Densher is not blind to the danger of his position, the potential violence in Kate, and he challenges her confidence: 'Then what can be so base as sacrificing me?'

In these early scenes, Kate confidently regards her plots as completely benign, even romantic. Her self-assurance is so complete that she answers Densher with the luxury of impatience in her voice:

> 'I shan't sacrifice you. Don't cry out till you're hurt. I shall sacrifice nobody and nothing, and that's just my situation, that I want and that I shall try for everything.'

This is only the second book of the first volume, but these words carry every indication of being famous last words. Of course, Kate is not intentionally dishonest here in that she is exactly right that she does want and try for everything. But we must wonder how she would regard herself if she could remember and repeat these words to herself at the end of the novel, knowing how many people she has so systematically sacrificed in her pursuit of 'everything.'

On the other hand, Milly Theale enters the London scene, and this heiress pursues not 'everything,' but 'something.' The difficulty in this is no less intense for the young American than it is for the handsome English girl, for Milly is as vague in her need for something as Kate is painfully clear about her need for everything. Kate has Densher, and accordingly, Milly has Susan Stringham, yet this does not present any sort of equilibrium, for the most profound interactions of the two pairs occur in a carefully arranged chiasm. Kate instructs Densher to 'be kind' to Milly; Milly is reciprocally made sympathetic to Densher, whom she believes is unsuccessfully in love with Kate. Kate, then, is tacitly allied with Mrs. Stringham's covert wishes to save Milly from her illness by having her fall in love with Densher. Indeed a union between Milly and Densher seems to appeal to most of James's characters in this novel, but all for different reasons. Kate's design perversely involves the marriage of her beloved to the dying heiress so that she may also gain the millions when she is reunited with Densher. Mrs. Stringham and Sir Luke believe that Milly needs love in order to fight for her life, and Mrs. Lowder is merely interested in whatever means would prevent the poor journalist from marrying her niece. Lord Mark, the aristocratic gold-digger, is the only dissenter to this proposal, especially after his own proposal to Milly fails. Here, James is endlessly subtle in his treatment of this failed suitor, whose opposition, unlike that of Mrs. Lowder, to Densher's apparently amorous intentions seems harmless but actually carried the fatal blow to Milly. Mrs. Lowder, whose powers had seemed great to the oppressed lovers, is comparatively passive and even inert as an agent against Kate and Densher. She does no outward damage, while the acutely blundering Lord Mark shatters Milly's utopian palazzo with his announcement of Kate and Densher's engagement.

It is a tribute to Milly that although the novel circles ceaselessly about her impending death, it is really never about her death at all. In that James is as generous to his character as she herself is to all the world. In fact, despite her great wealth, Milly's spiritual generosity is her one true extravagance, and such is the paradox that her generosity empties her and makes her a series of symbols. To Mrs. Stringham, Milly is a princess; to Kate and Densher, she is a dove. Even to herself, Milly is a symbol and she sheds tears of recognition to see a Bronzini portrait, whom she regards as a more honest version of herself in that it, a painting, assumes its inauthenticity and lifelessness by its very nature. In a rare moment of self-disclosure, which ends up to be yet another spacious vessel of her identity to be filled by her observers, Milly had said to her fellow traveler: 'Since I've lived all these years as if I were dead, I shall die, no doubt, as if I were alive—which will happen to be as you want me. So you see . . . you'll never really know where I am. Except indeed when I'm gone; and then you'll only know where I'm not.'

If *Wings of the Dove* is not about Milly, it is about Densher's gradual appreciation of the horrors of Kate's character. Kate herself is characteristically forthcoming about her weapons, lightly assuring Densher that her cleverness has 'grown infernal.' She is similarly unabashed of her rude handling of her lover in pawning him for Milly's gold:

> 'I want,' said the girl, 'to make things pleasant for her. I use, for the purpose, what I have. You're what I have of most precious, and you're therefore what I use most.'

For all her 'handsomeness,' Kate is, at last, a demonstration and the very embodiment of vulgarity. In awaiting the death of her friend, it is Kate who is the true vulture, not Mrs. Lowder, as Densher suggests early in the work. Kate is a unique type of scavenger in that she is also a predator, who carries off the sacrifices of life as a gift unto herself. Yet these are not her own sacrifices, but those of Milly and Densher, who suffer profoundly by her account. Indeed they suffer too much, and although Densher survives, he refuses to allow Kate to prey on him or Milly's memory at the end. His ultimatum—that she take him 'as he is' without the money that Milly has left to him or take the money without him—is his crucial moment of meeting Kate on her own battleground. In her pragmatism, however, Kate is unconquerable, and demonstrating no superfluous action or word even at this end, she merely shakes her head in the answer that sums it all: 'We shall never be again as we were!' ❀

List of Characters in
The Wings of the Dove

Milly Theale: An orphan and heiress from New York. Milly has a grave illness and does not have much time to live. Motivated by an intense passion to experience life to the fullest, she embarks on a journey to Europe. She is an immediate success, and it appears that there is nothing that she lacks. Yet ultimately, the absolutely bereaved American 'princess' wishes to experience love before she dies; this wish is the momentum that keeps her alive. Recognized as a 'dove' amongst the London circle that adopts her, Milly soundlessly, and apparently effortlessly, absorbs the entirety of the public and private projections of her friends into her person. In dying, as in living, Milly is 'splendid' in her absolute self-containment, and the dove spreads her great wings for the last time in her final bequest to Merton.

Kate Croy: Although perpetually 'handsome,' Kate is desperate to escape her sordid family background. In this, she has no choice but to allow her Aunt Maud to 'sponsor' her in London society; yet this agreement comes with a price, as this formidable sponsor does not approve of the man whom she loves. Kate, herself, is formidable in her determination to keep her love, and she performs the ultimate paradox in sacrificing even that love itself in her determination to execute her purpose. She is an essential pragmatist, and in the end, she betrays everyone but herself.

Merton Densher: Kate's lover, Densher is a penniless journalist, whose intelligence and charm are attractive even to the unlikely Mrs. Lowder. Although he is competent as a writer and intellectual, he is completely helpless in Kate's control, and he eventually realizes that he has allowed her to lead him too far into a place where he cannot conscientiously live. Made to engage in a false courtship of the dying Milly, Merton at last cannot reconcile his deception to his true heart, and demands that his lover take him 'as he is,' only to discover that he has found his resolve too late.

Aunt Maud Lowder: Kate's aunt is immediately associated with her possessions—the 'gilt, glass, satin, plush, rosewood, marble and malachite.' The scope of her persona is always grand, opaque, even cruel. Although she opposes Merton as a suitable match for her niece, she offers him genuine friendship, proving that she does not find it necessary even to bother raising an actual opposition against him. Like Kate, she is an essential pragmatist, and a more practiced one at that.

Susan Stringham: Lady writer from Boston who becomes Milly's confidante and companion-traveler to Europe. It is Mrs. Stringham who first regards Milly as a Princess, just as Kate first names her a Dove. Almost wholly indistinct in her own person, she completely devotes herself to the welfare of her young friend. She stands on another parallel with Kate in that she is a manipulator (although benign) behind Milly's every move.

Lord Mark: An epitome of the species of London's 'eligible bachelor,' Lord Mark hovers around Mrs. Lowder's receiving rooms in the hopes of catching either Kate or Milly. Quickly infatuated with the ethereal American princess, Lord Mark proposes to her, but is just as quickly refused. In an act that is only more stupid than it is cruel, he reveals Kate and Merton's engagement to Milly, who 'turns her face to the wall' at the news.

Sir Luke Strett: A renowned doctor who treats Milly while she is abroad. He is as sublimely subtle in his understanding of his patient as even Milly herself could wish, and he advises her explicitly to live, and implicitly to love, in order to really live. In return for his kindness to her, Milly consciously performs her acts of living at least for his benefit, and he remains devoted to his young patient to her grim end. ❀

Critical Views on
The Wings of the Dove

F. O. MATTHIESSEN ON *THE WINGS OF THE DOVE*

[F. O. Matthiessen (1902–1950) was Professor of History
and Literature at Harvard University. As a critic,
Matthiessen was interested in the history of American liter-
ature and the relationship of literature to society. His books
include *Translation: An Elizabethan Art, The Achievement of
T. S. Eliot,* and *American Renaissance.* He is the editor of
Selected Poems by Herman Melville and *Stories of Artists and
Writers by Henry James.* This excerpt from *Henry James: The
Major Phase* explicates the elaborate animal imagery found
in *The Wings of the Dove.*]

Shortly after this point James introduces the image that was to
become the symbol of his title. A more or less full account of this
image, of its morphology, so to speak, may help us to distinguish
James from the other symbolists. He is so fond of animal-imagery
of all sorts that it is hard to say whether, on the occasion when he
likens Aunt Maud to an eagle with 'gilded claws,' he is preparing
the way for the contrasting image of the dove, or is simply
responding to his painter's instinct to make every inch of his
canvas as lively as possible. For elsewhere Aunt Maud is a lioness, a
glossy embodiment of Britannia herself; just as, again, to Densher's
eyes, Milly, worn down by the social crush, becomes 'a Christian
maiden, in the arena, mildly, caressingly martyred,' not by the
nosing 'of lions and tigers but of domestic animals let loose as for
the joke.' But there would seem to be deliberate preparation of his
chief characterizing image for Milly in her own contrasting statement that she has used 'the wisdom of the serpent' to find in Sir
Luke Strett the special man for her need. For one quality of this
'dove' is that she is not so innocent as she looks. She may be fooled
by the new social complexity into which she has been plunged, she
may trustingly not suspect that Aunt Maud and Kate both have
designs upon her. But in the scene where the dove-image is introduced, she has her own strategy of how to play the part. Aunt
Maud has left the two girls together, with the request that Milly
find out for her whether Densher has returned yet from America.

One look at Kate virtually convinces Milly that he has. Then as Kate paces the room 'like a panther,' Milly is startled as at the foreboding of some sinister charged energy. It is when Kate becomes aware of Milly's strained feelings that she turns to her more gently and pronounces her 'a dove.' This speech serves to bring out again the contrast between the force and the delicacy of the two. But at that moment Aunt Maud reappears, whereupon Milly decides to appear at her 'most dovelike,' and yet to tell her, out of loyalty to Kate's unspoken secret, that she doesn't think Densher is back.

The next use of the image is during the great climactic scene in Venice, where Milly, her dress changed for the only time in the book from mourning robes to white, makes her most radiant appearance—and her last. As Kate and Densher stand watching her across the great room, a heavy 'priceless chain' of pearls around her neck, Kate says once again, 'She's a dove.' Densher agrees that the figure best describes Milly's spirit, but he then realizes how strongly the dove-like color of pearls also enters into Kate's impression. The power of wealth, he reflects, 'was dove-like only so far as one remembered that doves have wings and wondrous flights, have them as well as tender tints and soft sounds. It even came to him dimly that such wings could . . . spread themselves for protection. Hadn't they, for that matter, lately taken an inordinate reach, and weren't Kate and Mrs. Lowder, weren't Susan Shepherd and he, wasn't *he*, in particular, nestling under them to a great increase of immediate ease?' As Kate continues to dwell on the beauty of the pearls, he realizes with a twinge that 'pearls were exactly what Merton Densher would never be able to give her.' It is at this moment that Kate, who up until now has concealed the final range of her intention, comes out with her proposal that since Milly can't live, he is to marry her for her money. Just as Kate has delivered this proposal, Milly sends across the room to them 'all the candour of her smile.'

—F. O. Matthiessen, *Henry James: The Major Phase* (NY: Oxford University Press, 1944): pp. 68–70.

[Frederick C. Crews is Professor Emeritus of English at the University of California, Berkeley. His work includes *The Sins of the Fathers: Hawthorne's Psychological Themes, The Pooh Perplex: A Freshman Casebook, Out of My System: Psychoanalysis, Ideology, and Critical Method,* and *The Critics Bear It Away: American Fiction and the Academy.* This excerpt from *The Tragedy of Manners: Moral Drama in the Later Novels of Henry James* recounts the historical and personal influences that inspired James to create the characterization of Millie Theale in *The Wings of the Dove.*]

This may account in part for the striking differences in style between *The Ambassadors* and *The Wings of the Dove;* in the latter novel James was so familiar with his theme that he could deal with it almost entirely by indirection, by the contrast of symbols. Although *The Ambassadors, The Wings of the Dove,* and *The Golden Bowl* are usually taken together as representative of the later style, *The Ambassadors* only begins to suggest the resources of language that James employed in the two following novels. Method and meaning, which worked hand in glove in *The Ambassadors,* are often indistinguishable in *The Wings of the Dove.* The way things were said was important enough in *The Ambassadors,* but here things sometimes *are* the way they are said. Characters and idea simply do not exist for us apart from the images used to describe them. James's characters now conceive of everything—including each other—in terms of elaborate poetic analogies, and it gradually dawns on the reader that these analogies are all he really knows about any given character. Whereas in the earlier novels (*The Ambassadors* not excepted) the characters talked about events, here the events are often impossible to distinguish from the talk.

It will be seen that James had good dramatic reasons for this step toward abstraction, but regardless of his other motives it is certain that he saw the theme and central heroine of *The Wings of the Dove* as especially susceptible to such a treatment. "The idea, reduced to its essence," he wrote in the preface, "is that of a young person conscious of a great capacity for life, but early stricken and doomed, condemned to die under short respite, while also enamoured of the world; aware moreover of the condemnation and passionately desiring to 'put in' before extinction as many of the finer vibrations as possible, and so achieve, however briefly and brokenly, the sense of having lived." This is Milly Theale in the novel, but her prototype was Minny Temple, James's cousin. William and Henry James were both stunned when she died of tuberculosis in 1871; they called the event the end of their youth. The poignancy of Minny's fate—her love of life and her inability to stay alive—remained fixed in Henry's mind, and was further romanticized by his literary imagination. Even in her lifetime Minny had seemed to be merely the suggestion of a human being. In James's eyes she was so thoroughly buried by her sense of wasted opportunity that she had no distinguishable outlines at all. When he took her as a model for Isabel Archer in 1880–81, he felt her curious vagueness as an artistic drawback. He confided to Grace Norton: "Poor Minny was essentially incomplete—and I have attempted to make my young woman [Isabel] more rounded, more finished." However, by the time of *The Wings of the Dove* James was interested in roundness of a different sort, and now he saw Minny's indefiniteness as a positive advantage. In Milly Theale she became an indistinct, powerful symbol for life and loss, for beauty and the annihilation of beauty, and James deliberately refrained from "bringing her to life" in terms of everyday facts.

—Frederick C. Crews, *The Tragedy of Manners: Moral Drama in the Later Novels of Henry James* (New Haven, CT: Yale University Press, 1957): pp. 57–58.

LEO BERSANI ON THE NARRATOR AS CENTER IN THE NOVEL

[Leo Bersani is a retired Professor Emeritus in the Department of French at the University of California, Berkeley. Specializing in 19th- and 20th-century literature, his many works include *Marcel Proust: The Fictions of Life and of Art, The Death of Stéphane Mallarmé, Baudelaire and Freud,* and *Arts of Impoverishment: Beckett, Rothko and Resnais.* This excerpt from "The Narrator as Center in *The Wings of the Dove*" focuses on James's development of Merton Densher in his moral crisis and ultimatum regarding Kate Croy and Millie Theale.]

In the last third of the novel Milly becomes, for Densher, the opposite alternative from Kate. With him the drama of the self is enacted for the third time. Kate and Milly have, by their choices, become, allegorically, representatives of the way of the lioness and the way of the dove in Densher himself. The last books of the novel are the most dramatic; in them Densher's spirit is in the agonies of choice between the urgent appeals being made on him by both women. It is he who is really the central dramatic character of *The Wings of the Dove,* not merely because Milly tends to be rather a pale figure, but because it is the state of Densher's soul, "the question of the final stamp" to his personality, as James says, around which the moral action of the novel is built. His love for Kate is in one sense an illusion that he can deal with the world in her way. The crisis of his being is his revulsion at the methods of the lioness, and his gradual surrender to the dove-like in human nature.

But Densher's choice involves no essential change of personality. The novel shows his slow conscious recognition of his true self. He comes to recognize Milly as someone whose claims on him outweigh Kate's, and also as someone to whom he spontaneously responds. But he is really always more like Milly than like Kate. Both he and Milly, for example, are innocent about life. Milly comes to Europe with a prodigious thirst for experience of people, and Densher is presented as peculiarly deficient in awareness of life, as well as intensely eager to find himself involved in it. Kate appeals to him largely because he sees in her a talent for life, something he must arrange to "annex and possess."

But James's heroes and heroines seldom "annex and possess" life. They start out with a tremendous desire to do this, but they end with what is for them—and for James—the superior choice of renunciation. From the very beginning both Densher and Milly are strangers to the world of Lancaster Gate. Before a dinner party at Mrs. Lowder's, Densher thinks of Kate as an actress performing under the watchful eyes of her aunt, whom he sees as her "manager." He feels himself only on the edge of the drama being enacted between the two women; he has only his "purchased stall," is "relegated to mere spectatorship, a paying place in front, and one of the most expensive." But at Milly's party in Venice Densher feels himself "up to his neck" in the "wide warm waves" of Milly's special beauty, her "beatific mildness." Milly's beauty includes him in its aura, while

Kate's isolates him from her, makes him feel like an outsider at a frightening spectacle.

What should be pointed out is that Densher feels thus isolated from Kate's world even before Milly's influence begins to operate on him. There is very little development of character in *The Wings of the Dove*. James's centers, especially, are extensions of his own moral consciousness even when they have presumably not yet reached such a state of moral awareness. The choice of Milly as a spiritual direction to his life is implied in Densher's thoughts and feelings from the first moment we see him. For in James's mind the drama of the self's choice that he represents in Densher has already been enacted. What we have in the novel is a repetition, under the guise of independent, dramatic situations, of the moral choice of the mind from whose point of view the story is being narrated.

The *Wings of the Dove* is, then, largely about relations among different aspects of the narrator's mind. Now the conflicts among these aspects are resolved by purely mental processes, through reflection, assimilation, and rejection. But the framework of the novel's plot is an external, social one. Indeed, I am not at all sure, as Anderson seems to be, that James did not think of himself as having written a novel of social manners and morals; in his Preface to the novel he certainly does not recall any allegorical intention. And in the social world appreciation is only part of our response to others; it must, of course, be completed by action. But in *The Wings of the Dove* James pays attention only to inner response. The moral conflicts of the novel are resolved entirely in terms of new appreciations on the parts of the characters. I feel that as James wrote his story of a group of distinct individuals, he transformed it into a single inner drama of choice. Indeed, the plot itself of the drama seems to develop because of the needs of this drama of appreciation. The choice of the dove as the highest possibility of the self determines both the facts of the story and the point of view expressed toward them.

Densher moves from one moral allegiance to another without ever really disturbing the perfect stillness of his being. He recognizes Milly's appeal; he never acts on it. But his relationship with Milly necessarily involves him in alternatives of social action. And the merging of consciousness we have documented does not make for a community of moral agreement, not even, as Anderson would have it, between Milly and Densher as distinct individuals. The psychological and the social dramas are analogous in many respects, but the means and the natures of the resolutions are different, even irreconcilably opposed. There is in *The Wings of the Dove* a certain unresolved moral ambiguity even in the relationship which has presumably been perfected.

—Leo Bersani, "The Narrator as Center in *The Wings of the Dove,*" *Modern Fiction Studies* 6, no. 2 (Summer 1960): pp. 131–144.

BARBARA HARDY ON *THE WINGS OF THE DOVE*

[Barbara Hardy has written *Forms of Feeling in Victorian Fiction, Charles Dickens,* and *The Novels of George Eliot, a Study in Form.* This excerpt explores the notions of repudiation and redemption in James's characterization of Merton Densher.]

James's villains, as well as his heroine, are victims. Milly's riches doom her, and their desire for riches dooms them. James shows how the corruption of love and good will is slow and gradual, as events and people play into Kate's increasingly opportunistic hands. From the occasion when she manages things so that Densher drives out with Milly, to the last sexual transaction in Venice, we see the decline of her courage, spontaneity of passion, and delight in his mind, and his admiration of her. The move from free vitality to a controlled and artificial language and behaviour is like Gwendolen Harleth's loss of spirit and fun after her marriage to Grandcourt. Here we see a relationship corrupted, a waste and destruction of a rare loving affinity, and the takeover of love by transaction and blackmail. The tragic loss is one for the lovers too, as true and truthful love is compromised and lost by false play.

The most puzzling member of the creative triad is Merton Densher, not so much because his succumbing is implausible, as Tony Tanner says (in his *Henry James*) but because of the handling of his change of heart. This change is confirmed by one of James's functional characters, Susan Shepherd Stringham, a successfully particularized agent. When she tells Densher about the revelations which make Milly turn her face to the wall, there is an uncomfortable dialogue full of characteristically pregnant pauses and telepathy, a conversation in every sense, in which Susan's assumptions that he must be on Milly's side bring him over. Despite the simplifications in theological readings (for example, Dorothea Krook's in *The Ordeal of Consciousness in Henry James*), there is no doubt that the novel relies on a Christian ethic, like *Macbeth* and *Othello*. Densher is a Catholic, whose visit to the Brompton Oratory at Christmas after Milly's death strongly suggests that he is a penitent sinner, but though Milly is his redeemer, she is too particularized as American heiress and tragic victim to be a Christ figure. Susan Shepherd Stringham is also reduced and dehumanized by being read as Christ, but there is a touch of the good shepherd about her, shown most effectively in her thorough Jamesian telepathic expectations of Densher. Christian theology is present, but it is a novel which works as a humanist text also, old and new moralities coinciding as Densher meets a new self-image in Susan's humane faith. The corruptibility of love and relationship, and the historical construction of their corruption, are more complex and touching than religious readings suggest. But the moral processes are not always clear.

There is a certain glossing-over of Densher's conduct to Milly. The condemnation of Lord Mark comes more acceptably from Susan than from him. Mark is cruel and stupid in telling Milly about the attachment of Kate and Densher, but Densher's judgement is strikingly unaccompanied by self-blame. ⟨. . .⟩

Densher demonstrates his change of heart, and though there is still no self-reproach there is no need for it. It is present in what happens. The rejection of marriage with Kate on her terms, and his rejection of Milly's bequest, is a conclusive moral act. The famous line 'We shall never be again as we were' articulates the loss of their virtue and the loss of their love, which Kate laments as she recognizes that he is 'in love' with Milly's 'memory', her conventional words for his developed sense of Milly's 'reality', which she reads as from far off. When he offered marriage 'as they were', it may look as if Densher is bargaining again with Kate, but there is no question of his terms being accepted and the transactions of love are repudiated, as they are in *King Lear*, unromantically. The novel knows and shows that they were comprehensible.

—Barbara Hardy, *Henry James: The Later Writing* (UK: Northcote House Publishers Ltd., 1996): pp. 47–50.

KEVIN KOHAN ON VICTIMS OF METAPHOR IN
THE NOVEL

[Kevin Kohan is a Lecturer in the Department of English at
the University of British Columbia. His essay "Victims of
Metaphor in *The Wings of the Dove*" appeared in *The Henry
James Review,* and an essay on *The Golden Bowl* is forthcoming in *Studies in the Novel.* In progress is a book-length
study of late-19th century American realism. Kohan discusses the power of metaphor in James's characterization of
Millie Theale in this selection.]

Milly is quickly positioned for exploitation. Shortly after her arrival in
London, she considers herself lost in a labyrinth of alien motives and
complications, the most mysterious of which seem to be indicated by
the way she has herself become such a smashing success. Although her
own view is that she is "in a current determined, through her indifference, timidity, bravery, generosity—she could scarce say which—by
others," Kate tells her, "You're an outsider, independent and standing
by yourself; you're not hideously relative to tiers and tiers of others."
Positioning Milly beyond the current of relations—rejecting Milly's
own naturalistic, linear image for a social, hierarchical one—Kate
applies the metaphor that provides her plot with its pretext: she tells
Milly that she is a dove, and the effect on Milly is profound:

> [Hearing it] she felt herself ever so delicately, so consider-
> ately, embraced; not with familiarity or as a liberty taken,
> but almost ceremonially and in the manner of an *accolade;*
> partly as if, though a dove who could perch on a finger, one
> were also a princess with whom forms were to be observed
> . . . It was, moreover, for the girl, like an inspiration: she
> found herself accepting as the right one, while she caught
> her breath with relief, the name so given her. She met it on
> the instant as she would have met revealed truth; it lighted
> up the strange dusk in which she lately had walked. *That*
> was what was the matter with her. She was a dove.

Milly's "matter" here undergoes a radical displacement, the word no
longer referring to her physical condition. The name "ceremoni-
ously" given her, a "revealed truth" and an "inspiration," defines her
being ("She was a dove"), signaling a powerfully appropriating
translation. Significantly, the metaphor functions, for Milly, in what

could be called a lateral fashion. Its radical power originates in its ability to refer, almost instantaneously, to another image. If Milly is a "dove," she is also "a princess with whom forms were to be observed." "Observed" must be given a double valence—Milly calls forth the courtly manners of fairy tales, and Milly is herself the site of forms where the play of structure is made evident. Indeed, Susan remarks that Milly "liv[es] for the most part, in such an appeased way, on the plane of mere elegant representation."

When the princess-dove finds suitable lodgings in the unreal, de-materializing Venetian palace—which holds "its history still in its great lap, even like a painted idol, a solemn puppet hung about with decorations"—she is further absorbed into the realm of metaphor. First she is said to roam her palace "slowly to and fro as the priestess of the worship," and then these three figures—princess-dove-priestess—are yoked together to create a version of Milly so image-ridden as to be less a representational marker than an empty site across which such markers chaotically flow. James here pulls the narrative focus away from the consciousness-frame and draws the reader to the narrator's view; the culminating fusion indicated by this triple image is not available to anyone within the text's world: "[W]e have positively the image, in the delicate dusk, of the figure so associated and yet so opposed, so mutually watchful: that of the angular pale princess, ostrich-plumed, black-robed, hung about with amulets, reminders, relics, mainly seated, mainly still." The priestess is now represented by an elaborated synecdoche: she wears black robes over-laden with the trinkets of history. Under the force of the accumulation of metaphors, the originating metaphor can be trans-formed—James, satirizing the slippage of metaphors, permits the dove to become the ostrich—as though the first metaphor is itself usurped by metaphor. Milly is entirely at the disposal of whatever would name her. Indeed she is held fast by these metaphors, activated, through James's ironic prose, only by two verb phrases—"mainly seated, mainly still"—that waver between reference to the princess figure and to the amulets and relics that she wears: she or what she wears is almost immobile. The distinction is destabilized because it is virtually irrelevant—the wearer and the worn are both mere images.

—Kevin Kohan, "Victims of Metaphor in *The Wings of the Dove*," *Henry James Review* 20, no. 2 (1999): pp. 135–154.

[Gary Kuchar is a doctoral candidate at McMaster University. He has published articles on literary theory and Renaissance literature in *Mosaic, Canadian Review of Contemporary Literature, Early Modern Literary Studies*, and *Journal of Narrative Theory*. In this excerpt, Kuchar contrasts the consciousnesses of Kate Croy and Millie Theale as each woman regards herself in the novel.]

James is explicit in the passage from the 1910 essay that the process of making "speculative and imaginative connections," of taking up "conceived presumptions and pledges" concludes, when at its most authentic, by transforming "*the fields of experience*" from which the process itself arose. Indeed, James is deeply concerned with how various modes of representation reflect differing existential comportments to the world and the possibilities of self-transformation which arise therein. This process of construing imaginative connections is central to the construction of the main characters in *The Wings of the Dove*—particularly Kate Croy and Milly Theale. It will be my principal challenge in this essay then to illustrate that the existentially distinguishable comportments towards the world of Kate in Book One and Milly in Books Four and Five emerge through significant differences in the styles of each section. These shifts in form reveal that Kate's perception is *impoverished,* in a Heideggarian sense, insofar as it is saturated by the material conditions around her. This impoverishment-of-world, this sense that she does not form a completely individuated self—but is held prisoner by her past—is conveyed stylistically through a highly ambiguous and often discontinuous narrative. Such ambiguity and discontinuity places Kate at a distance from both the narrator and the reader, suggesting that she is not entirely self-coherent, not, in other words, fully individuated. Milly, on the other hand, is far less rooted in the past as she moves towards deeper and deeper self-awareness until her consciousness is fully disclosed to herself and to the reader in Book Five. This process of coming into greater self-consciousness results in increasingly more intense levels of intimacy between her and the reader. This intimacy becomes most intense during the Regnet's Park scene, as Milly realizes a profound "consciousness of relations" through a recognition of her own mortality. ⟨. . .⟩

Kate's unease with the world is first manifested in the extraordinarily dense prose of the novel's opening. The repetition of her name following the second person pronoun sets the hesitant tone for Kate's perception of Lionel Croy's "vulgar little room" and the "deeper depth" each object in it signifies to her. This opening also presents the first in a series of images that offer a mirrored or painted reflection of a character. While waiting for her father, "there were moments at which she [Kate] showed herself, in the glass over the mantel, a face positively pale with irritation." Kate does not catch a glimpse of herself, she does not see herself unintentionally, but rather she "shows herself" in fragmentary and spectralizing gestures. The emphasis here is on Kate's tendency to guard against self-disclosure. This subtle and obfuscated moment of cautious exposure contrasts with Milly's eventual recognition of her mortality in the Bronzino scene and the subsequent sense of intimacy with the world that emerges from visions of each other, while providing enough context to overcome such misprision. ⟨. . .⟩

During her first appearance in the novel Kate looks at her reflection and is described as having "*lost herself* in the thought of the way she might still pull things round had she only been a man." This loss of self expresses the sense that her world absorbs her; its materiality encompasses her being in such a manner that she is disposed to the world in a mode of everydayness and inauthenticity. Her consciousness is not focused on the ways that the necessary conditions, or existential limits, reveal possibilities, but rather on wishing itself out of those limits. This comportment to the world, which is solidified by Kate's meeting with her father, is expressed most clearly following the meeting when "she saw as she had never seen before how material things spoke to her." As the opening of the novel reveals, the material world has always spoken to Kate; now she does not resist hearing it.

—Gary Kuchar, "Henry James and the Phenomenal Reader: Consciousness and the Variation of Style in *The Wings of the Dove*," *Henry James Review* 21, no. 2 (2000): pp. 170–185.

Plot Summary of
The Ambassadors

The problem of place is the point of departure for this novel that James considered his most perfect. As the story begins, however, the problem is made quite simple. Chad Newsome has taken up residence in Paris, and despite his family's correspondences to return home, he has not and has even ceased addressing their pleas. Here, then, is the stark divide—Paris and Woollett, Massachusetts; Chad and Mrs. Newsome. The original problem becomes more complex as the mother's desperation drives her to send her informal fiancé, Lambert Strether, to recall her son. And here, F. W. Dupee best sums up the complication: "American ambassadors are notoriously susceptible." For although Strether travels to Europe as Mrs. Newsome's ambassador of Woollett, Chad himself demonstrates a more skillful ambassadorship in that Strether is converted to his side of the ocean with hardly a scuffle of resistance.

Evidently, the once rough-hewn teenager of provincial New England has learned more than just the social graces of conversation and dress. He has become an impressive connoisseur of tact such that he does not even allow himself to be seen by his mother's ambassador until the latter has had some time of exposure to the charms of Paris. Fortunately for Chad, the older man is socially innocent and extremely impressionable; the vivacity of Paris is not lost on him, therefore, and Chad has largely won over the ambassador even before their reunion. In fact, Strether seems to recognize his need for mental and spiritual liberation from the first day of his arrival in the Old World. His self-revelatory remark to his newfound companion, Miss Gostrey, is heavily tinged with a wistful desire for immediacy in his life:

> 'You did put your finger on it a few minutes ago. It's general, but it avails itself of particular occasions. That's what it's doing for me now. I'm always considering something else; something else, I mean, than the thing of the moment. The obsession of the other thing is the terror.'

Thus, in spite of his provincialism, and because of his frustration at the limits of that life, Strether is unknowingly prepared for a significant shift. This moment occurs in the luxurious gardens of the celebrated sculptor, Gloriani, and the customarily reserved Strether is seized by an inspiration for life.

> Live all you can . . . It doesn't so much matter what you
> do . . . so long as you had your life. . . . Live!

There is nothing of the Puritanism of Woollett in this speech; surely Mrs. Newsome would never agree with such a philosophy that discards the mode and method by which one should live. Yet Strether experiences an exhilaration of realization such that finally his life becomes to him real and present. Still, we cannot expect that the man is wholly altered; his idealism is perhaps now more enhanced than ever before, and in his enthusiasm for his new surroundings, Strether wants very much to believe that Chad is living a life that is as virtuous as it is elegant. At this point, he is not prepared to appreciate or accept Mme de Vionnet, who, in her foreignness, is still too imbibed with the Woollett-born presupposition that Chad remains in Europe at the side of a sordid woman. Consequently, he decides that it must be her daughter, Jeanne, in whom Chad has placed his love that ties him to the Old World away from his family in Woollett.

Meanwhile, Strether himself has been long absent from Woollett, and his patroness does not display the subtlety that her son did in such a situation. First ceasing correspondence with her fiancé, she sends a second platoon of ambassadors, this time more fully reenforced. Sarah Pocock, her daughter and younger version of herself, Jim, Sarah's husband, and Mamie, Jim's sister and Chad's hopeful wife-to-be, form the triple force of this second envoy. Demanded to renounce Mme de Vionnet and immediately return with them to Woollett, Strether confirms his alienation of Mrs. Newsome and Woollett when he fails to satisfy Sarah's demands. He seems to be burning whatever tenuous bridge that may remain to connect him to his hometown across the ocean when he goes so far as to explicitly advise Chad to remain in Paris with the charming mother and daughter de Vionnets. As far as Strether understands Chad's situation, the young man owes the Madame a great debt for his social education, and the older man considers that it would be a great shame on Chad's part to abandon her daughter, in whom he is presumably interested.

In characteristically Jamesian form, the climax of the novel occurs in the natural beauty and calm of a French riverside resort, as

Strether is confronted with the coincidental arrival of Chad and Mme de Vionnet on a rowboat. They are alone, and had evidently planned to enjoy a lovers' retreat at the nearby inn. No longer can Strether support his idea of the budding love affair between Chad and Jeanne, for obviously he is indulging in an adulterous affair with her mother, and again the Woollett-trained moralist is forced to make a decision. It is a testament to Strether's determination to live that he does not retract his loyalty to Mme de Vionnet, but rather decides that he actually respects the heroism in her refusal to allow social embarrassment to disrupt their mutual friendship. Even after they both realize Chad's real desire to return to the comfort of manufacturing in Woollett, Strether's primary sympathies remain with Mme de Vionnet who he all too clearly recognizes has given much but gained nothing from her beloved.

Perhaps it is because of this respect for Mme de Vionnet's generosity to Chad, coupled with his recent liberation from the oppressive competence of Mrs. Newsome in managing his life, that Strether cannot conscientiously agree to Maria Gostrey's implied marriage proposal. He could not live, as it were, in Woollett because Mrs. Newsome's convenient social and business arrangement made himself useless to his own life. Having gained so much from his ironic stint as ambassador to Europe, Strether foresees that marrying Miss Gostrey would again cause his own irrelevance to himself, and he is quite willing to sacrifice the comforts of marriage for the continued privilege to really live. Thus his final conversation with Maria rings a note of personal ambition to take on the world anew with nothing but his newfound life. ❀

List of Characters in
The Ambassadors

Lambert Strether: A widower of age fifty-five, who despite his age, is extremely innocent about the world. He is an editor of a minor literary magazine. At the request of his patroness and fiancée, Mrs. Newsome, he embarks to Europe to bring back to Woollett, Massachusetts, her son, who she believes is leading a dissolute life there. However, Strether's impression of Europe is wholly outside of his self-righteous expectations, and he comes to recognize the wisdom and beauty of the Old World in spite of himself. With his altered conscience, Strether's decisions in Europe are made on behalf of what he perceives as love and personal integrity rather than duty, sacrificing his relationship with Mrs. Newsome in his renewed sense of life and himself.

Mrs. Newsome: A prominent and wealthy widow of Woollett, Massachusetts. She is defined by her moral zeal and habitual charity, which, to her, seem to justify the large fortune and thriving manufacturing business that she has inherited from her late husband. She is never physically present in the action of the novel; however, her influence is a constant and ominous pressure for her son and her various 'ambassadors' to Europe.

Chad Newsome: Strether remembers Chad to have been a headstrong and coarse young man in Massachusetts. However, his residence in Europe has much refined his manner so that he is an elegant gentleman. Despite his changed appearance, however, Chad seems to have retained the brutish qualities of his youth, and Strether is finally appalled at the younger man's refusal to take responsibility for his intimate relationship with Mme de Vionnet in light of the advantages offered by his mother in taking over the lucrative family business.

Mme Marie de Vionnet: A charming lady friend of Chad Newsome. She is separated but not divorced from her husband, and it is later revealed that she is Chad's lover who is responsible for his social improvements in Europe. Mme de Vionnet is helplessly—and rather commonly—in love with Chad, although she knows that he will eventually leave her and return to America to make a respectable match and continue the family business. Strether, vaguely in love with her himself, promises to 'save her' by preventing Chad's return to America.

Jeanne de Vionnet: Mme de Vionnet's young daughter, who Strether initially believes is the object of Chad's love. Exquisite and sweet, Jeanne is the apple of her mother's eye and the epitome of the fresh European debutante. She eventually marries the French nobleman that Chad and her mother arrange for her.

Maria Gostrey: Strether's consistent confidante, whom he haphazardly meets upon his arrival to Chester. Miss Gostrey, who is technically American, but has internalized the national character of Europe, presents the perpetually confused Strether with lighthearted revelations of the truth. She eventually falls in love with Strether and tacitly proposes that he remain in Europe with her.

Waymarsh: Strether's initial liaison in Europe. Waymarsh is a successful New England businessman who is forced to reside in Europe following some great mental stress. Waymarsh is the male personification of New World austerity, which James terms 'the sacred rage,' and he remains a satiric figure throughout the novel.

Sarah Pocock: Chad's married sister who leads the second round of 'ambassadors' to Europe after Strether's apparent failure to complete his mission. A lesser substitute for her mother, Sarah represents the strict provincial morality of Woollett. She refuses to appreciate Europe, Mme de Vionnet, or even her brother's improvements by any means.

Jim Pocock: Sarah Pocock's husband. He is a foolish and coarse individual who confirms Strether's newfound realizations regarding the nature of his hometown.

Mamie Pocock: Jim's sister. A beautiful girl in her own right, she is the family's choice for Chad to marry. Although she is quite young, Mamie already exudes the maternal patience of Puritan New England, and understanding that Chad has already undergone improvement under a female influence, she does not insist on her claim to him.

Little Bilham: A friend of Chad. He is Strether's first taste of Chad's much refined lifestyle. Also an American, Little Bilham came to Paris to paint, but has since abandoned his art from lack of confidence.

Gloriani: A famous sculptor, whose home and gardens greatly impress Strether in its grand scope of luxury and extravagance. Gloriani is extremely successful financially by his art, and he lives a reckless lifestyle surrounded by glitz and beautiful women. The utter absence of Puritan mores strikes the American visitor as foreign as it is exhilarating. ❀

Critical Views on
The Ambassodors

PERCY LUBBOCK ON THE CRAFT OF FICTION

[Percy Lubbock (1879–1965), novelist, essayist, and biographer, edited James's letters in 1920 and wrote *The Craft of Fiction,* one of the seminal studies of modern fictional techniques. His other works include *Roman Pictures, Shades of Eton,* and *Portrait of Edith Wharton.* This selection from *The Craft of Fiction* argues that James's Lambert Strether in *The Ambassadors* stands as an example of a fictional character that is distinctly autonomous from its author.]

If it should still be doubted, however, whether the right use of autobiography is really so limited, it might be a good answer to point to Henry James's Strether, in *The Ambassadors;* Strether may stand as a living demonstration of all the autobiography cannot achieve. He is enough to prove finally how far the intricate performance of thought is beyond the power of a man to record in his own language. Nine-tenths of Strether's thought—nine-tenths, that is to say, of the silvery activity which makes him what he is—would be lost but for the fact that its adventures are caught in time, while they are proceeding, and enacted in the book. Pictured by him, as he might himself look back on them, they would drop to the same plane as the rest of the scene, the picture of the other people in the story; his state of mind would figure in his description on the same terms as the world about him, it would simply be a matter for him to describe like another. In the book as it is, Strether personally has nothing to do with the impression that is made by the mazy career of his imagination, he has no hand in the effect it produces. It speaks for itself, it spreads over the scene and colours the world just as it did for Strether. It is immediately in the foreground, and the "seeing eye" to which it is presented is not his, but the reader's own.

No longer a figure that leans and looks out of a window, scanning a stretch of memory—that is not the image suggested by Henry James's book. It is rather as though the reader himself were at the window, and as though the window opened straight into the depths of Strether's conscious existence. The energy of his perception and discrimination is there seen at work. His mind is the mirror of the scene beyond it, and the other people in the book exist only in relation to him; but his mind, his own thought of them, is there absolutely, its restless evolution is in full sight. I do not say that this is a complete account of the principle on which the book is constructed; for indeed the principle goes further, encompassing points of method to be dealt with later. But for the moment let the book stand as the type of the novel in which a mind is dramatized—reflecting the life to which it is exposed, but itself performing its own peculiar and private life. This last, in the case of Strether, involves a gradual, long-drawn change, from the moment when he takes up the charge of rescuing his young friend from the siren of Paris, to the moment when he finds himself wishing that his young friend would refuse to be rescued. Such is the curve in the unexpected adventure of his imagination. It is given as nobody's view—not his own, as it would be if he told the story himself, and not the author's, as it would be if Henry James told the story. The author does not tell the story of Strether's mind; he makes it tell itself, he dramatizes it.

—Percy Lubbock, *The Craft of Fiction* (NY: Viking Press, 1957): pp. 142–71.

F. O. MATTHIESSEN ON *THE AMBASSADORS*

[F. O. Matthiessen (1902–1950) was Professor of History and Literature at Harvard University. As a critic, Matthiessen was interested in the history of American literature and the relationship of literature to society. His books include *Translation: An Elizabethan Art, The Achievement of T. S. Eliot,* and *American Renaissance.* He is the editor of *Selected Poems by Herman Melville* and *Stories of Artists and Writers by Henry James.* This selection discusses the structural achievement of James in maneuvering within the limits of serialized fiction to effect dramatic tension and suspense in *The Ambassadors.*]

What caused James's preference for the book was not its theme, but its roundness of structure. On the same grounds of "'architectural' competence" his second favorite was *The Portrait of a Lady*. In *The Ambassadors* we have a fine instance of the experienced artist taking an external convention, and, instead of letting it act as a handicap, turning it to his own signal advantage. James had always been uneasy—as well he might have been!—with his age's demand for serialized fiction. But here for once he felt a great stimulus to his ingenuity, and he laid out his novel organically in twelve books, each of which could serve for a month's installment. His subject was well fitted to such treatment, since it consisted in Strether's gradual initiation into a world of new values, and a series of small climaxes could therefore best articulate this hero's successive discoveries. It is interesting to note also the suspense that James creates by the device of the delayed introduction of the chief characters in Strether's drama.

The opening book at Chester, where Strether, arriving from Liverpool to meet his friend Waymarsh, encounters first Maria Gostrey, is really a prologue that strikes the theme of Europe—the Europe of old houses and crooked streets which was also being stamped upon American imaginations by James's contemporary, Whistler. The second book begins in London, and though Strether is already started on his eager growth through fresh impressions, how far he still has to go is indicated by Maria's remark that the theater which he takes "for—comparatively divine" is "impossible, if you really want to know." During this conversation Chad Newsome's name is first casually introduced, and then followed by expertly swift exposition of the situation which Strether has come out to rectify. But we don't see Chad himself for some time yet. Strether must have his initial taste of Paris, that "vast bright Babylon." As he stands in the Boulevard Malesherbes looking up at the balcony of Chad's apartment, he recognizes in a flash, in the essence of Jamesian revelation, that the life which goes on in such balanced and measured surroundings cannot possibly be the crude dissipation that Woollett, Massachusetts, believes. His initiation has reached its crucial stage. ⟨. . .⟩

⟨. . .⟩ James has already conceived what sacrifice that will mean for his hero, that he will lose "the strenuous widow," whom he was to have married, "and all the advantages attaching to her." "It is too late, too late *now* for *him* to live—but what stirs in him with a dumb passion of desire, of I don't know what, is the sense that he may have a little supersensual hour in the vicarious freedom of another." The signal omission from this outline is any mention of Madame de Vionnet. The transformation of that phrase, "of I don't know what," into the richest source of Strether's awakening is one token of how much James's final themes accrued by the years in which he let his imagination play over them before bringing them to completion.

—F. O. Matthiessen, "The Ambassadors," *The Question of Henry James: A Collection of Critical Essays* edited by F. W. Dupee (NY: Henry Holt and Company, Inc., 1945): pp. 218-223.

JOHN E. TILFORD JR. ON JAMES THE OLD INTRUDER

[In this selection, Tilford opposes Percy Lubbock's famous argument in *The Craft of Fiction,* which separated James and his character Strether as two distinct voices. By noting deviations from this claim, Tilford holds that the narrative conventions of the Victorian novel are not wholly absent from James's writing in *The Ambassadors.*]

The Ambassadors has long been acclaimed the Master's supreme example of the single point of view—"of employing but one centre," as he puts it, "and keeping it all within my hero's compass." Strether's consciousness was to be projected upon his "intimate adventure . . . from beginning to end without intermission or deviation," and it was "Strether's sense" of all other characters, "and Strether's only," that was to be shown.

Admirers of James have borne ardent witness to the glorious fulfilment of this intention. Foremost is Percy Lubbock, in his widely esteemed *Craft of Fiction* (New York, 1921). Lubbock particularly emphasizes James's withdrawal, his standing aside, "to let Strether's thought tell its own story." ⟨. . .⟩

An examination of the text itself, however, indicates that the centre is by no means always kept within the "hero's compass" and that often the novel does pass "outside the circle of his thought." Quite frequently the author interposes "with a vision of his own," and he has not, like a playwright, vanished altogether. And the authorial intrusions are certainly not restricted to the first chapter, but continue throughout the novel. One of James's obvious intrusions, for instance, is the naming of his "centre." Many times he refers to his protagonist, with kindly archness, as "poor Strether," "poor man," and at least once as "our hero." More noticeable is his frequent designation of Strether as "our friend," sometimes twice on a page. This phrase occurs more than sixty-five times; familiar in nineteenth-century fiction, it inevitably implies an amiable understanding between the candid narrator and his gentle reader.

More significant is James's frequent appearance as the editorially omniscient author, speaking frankly in the first person, taking his reader into his confidence about his characters and about his own part in telling the story. On the opening page he writes: "The principle I have just mentioned . . ." and later he speaks of Strether's prolonging "the meditation I describe." Again and again one notes such phrases as "incidents with which we have yet to make acquaintance," "as we know," "as I have called it," "briefer than our glance at the picture," "if we might so far discriminate," and "we have just seen." ⟨. . .⟩

Lapses and shifts of this nature may be thought relatively minor; and it might have been difficult for James or anyone else at this time completely to avoid them. But the point is that they are present, and pervasively so, and that they are inconsistencies in his method.

James's deviations from his ideal technique, furthermore, also involve shifts of point of view from Strether's to other characters'. These are the most difficult of all to perceive, for it is here that the Master's art of concealment is most splendidly subtle. These shifts are not abundant, and they do not last long; but they too are nonetheless present. ⟨. . .⟩

Henry James, it is hence fair to state, fulfilled rather less consistently than he thought his intention "of employing but one centre and keeping it all within [his] hero's compass," of projecting Strether's consciousness upon his experiences "from beginning to end without intermission or deviation," and of availing himself of "Strether's sense of these things, and Strether's only . . . for showing them." The authorial intrusion and the shifts of point of view are sufficiently abundant to modify his claim. Moreover, unqualified critical claims like those quoted earlier clearly need toning down.

The author has not completely withdrawn; Strether's thought does not tell *all* "its own story"; the subject does not consist "entirely" of his impressions; we do see many interpositions of authorial visions; James does not "most carefully [refrain] from using his knowledge"; and, far from having vanished, the author is very much present, frequently "addressing us" and "reporting his impression to the reader."

—John E. Tilford Jr., "James The Old Intruder," *Modern Fiction Studies* 4, no. 2 (Summer 1958): pp. 157–164.

GRANVILLE H. JONES ON LAMBERT STRETHER AND THE PAST RECAPTURED

[Granville H. Jones was Professor Emeritus of English and American literature at Carnegie-Mellon University. He is the author of *Henry James' Psychology of Experience*. His other works are largely on Jack Kerouac. In this excerpt, Professor Jones discusses the initial innocence and gradual awakening of Strether's consciousness in his exposure to the Old World.]

Lambert Strether's consciousness is both voracious and vulnerable. It seeks and savors impressions; it is teased and bombarded and pulverized by them. It is composed of a "too interpretative innocence", according to James, and an exhaustive sense of responsibility. Its accretions and responses are the sum of the content and the form of *The Ambassadors*.

Strether's innocence, however, is a relative state. Of equal important are, on the one hand, his prejudices and his ignorance and, on the other hand, his susceptibilities and his acuteness. Through gaining perspective he recognizes the shallow limitations and false assumptions of his New England moral code and, by a subtle reversal, regains the purity he does not know he has lost. Writing of Strether, Cargill says, "He is an innocent, an idealist . . . , and this is his major limitation as he arrives in Europe on his appointed task." Insofar as the "appointed task" is motivated by suspicion, shortsightedness, and Puritan prudery, this is true. Like Mrs. Newsome,

Sarah Pocock, and anyone else who is a product of the Woollett, Massachusetts, moral order, Strether is predisposed to believe that Chad is being corrupted by a corrupt woman. Only as he is purged of this prejudice, which is antithetical to clear vision and innocence as well, does Strether become a free and innocent idealist.

The process is a complicated one involving Strether's total sensibilities. Like all the great initiatees in James's fiction, Strether has his guides and his confidante. Unlike most of them, however, Strether does not have his intimate affections or his expectations abused or betrayed. He is lied to, but the lies are like Mrs. Lowder's "proper lie" in *The Wings of the Dove* and Fanny's and the Prince's necessary lies in *The Golden Bowl:* Strether must not be told the naked truth until he has matured enough to understand its equivocations; he must be deluded for his own good. Like a recalcitrant spectator at a play, he must have his disbelief suspended for him by the simple device of the actors telling him that what he is seeing is real, it is true, it is *only* what it appears to be. ⟨. . .⟩

With conscience and its concomitant guilt filed neatly away as New England anachronisms, Strether's moral concerns slide to the periphery of his consciousness while his aesthetic, social, and emotional senses dominate his mind. True, he is always aware of his responsibility to Mrs. Newsome—his obligation to see to it that Chad abandons his woman and leaves Paris—yet with the situation different from what he expected, Strether finds both his duty less easily defined and his responsibility more distractedly scattered. Unaware of how much he is being affected, Strether is engulfed by life while he thinks he is merely observing it. When he tells little Bilham, "Live all you can"; when he recognizes at Chad's party that "such an occasion as this . . . isn't the people. It's what has made the people possible"; when he shocks Sarah by declaring that Woollett's "general state of mind had proceeded, on its side, from our queer ignorance, our queer misconceptions and confusions"; when he accepts Marie de Vionnet even after he has learned that her attachment to Chad is indeed a sexual liaison—these are the buds, the blossoms, and the final fruition of Strether's maturation.

—Granville H. Jones, *Henry James' Psychology of Experience: Innocence, Responsibility, and Renunciation in the Fiction of Henry James* (Netherlands: Mouton & Co., 1975): pp. 262–264.

MARTHA C. NUSSBAUM ON STRAIGHTNESS AND SURPRISE

[Martha C. Nussbaum is Ernst Freund Professor of Law and Ethics at the University of Chicago. She is the author of many books, including *Poetic Justice, The Fragility of Goodness,* and *Cultivating Humanity.* In this excerpt from *Love's Knowledge,* Professor Nussbaum focuses on the unique characterization of Mrs. Newsome, whose presence is felt throughout *The Ambassadors* even in her absolute absence from the action of the novel.]

James's richly comic portrait of Mrs. Newsome lies at the center of his story of Strether's adventure. Present vividly in her absence, she articulates, by contrast, Strether's moral movement. He begins as her ambassador, the agent of her antecedently fixed moral purpose; he ends as a child "toddling" alone, a diver in depths, a hearer of strange and crowded voices, a floater upon inexorable tides of light. To understand Strether's struggle we must understand *her*—and with a certain sympathy: asking how, for example, her refusal of surprise "falls in" with the fact that she is all fine cold thought; asking, too, why her vision of life appeals to our friend and stirs, as it continually does, his moral imagination.

We notice first and most obviously her moralism, her preoccupation with questions of moral right and wrong, with criticism of offense, with judgment upon vice. "Essentially all moral pressure," as Strether describes her, she motivates his own obsession with discipline and punishment, his determination "always, where Lambert Strether was concerned, to know the worst." Indeed he is attracted to her, perhaps, just because of "his old tradition, the one he had been brought up on and which even so many years of life had but little worn away; the notion that the state of the wrongdoer, or at least this person's happiness, presented some special difficulty." It is no accident that her principles are for him, embodied in the dream figure of a judging mother who "loom(s) at him larger than life" until "he already felt her come down on him, already burned under her reprobation, with the blush of guilt. . . . He saw himself, under her direction, recommitted to Woollett as juvenile offenders are committed to reformatories." To her obsession with the priority of moral right, which fills, it seems, the entirety of her exalted consciousness (the presence of moral pressure is "almost identical with her own presence,") we may add rigorism in her conception of principles. Everything in her world must be "straight" (Strether, later, calls her "the whole moral and intellectual being or block"); and her rules of right admit of no softening in the light of the present circumstance, the individual case. "She was the only woman he had known, even at Woollett, as to whom his conviction was positive that to lie was beyond her art": she "refused to human commerce that mitigation of rigor." Strether links his thought of her with the idea of an exceptionless justice that dwells outside "in the hard light." This moral rigorism, together with the ubiquity of moral assessment, permits her two attitudes only, when confronted with a new occurrence: approval or disapproval. "From the moment they're not delighted," Strether says of her and her new Ambassador Sarah, "they can only be—well what I admit she was."

If universal and general principles of right take precedence over (and indeed swallow up) all other elements of life, there are three aspects of human experience that Mrs. Newsome especially dislikes and avoids: emotion, passivity, and the perception of particularity. These items are connected in an interesting and, in a certain sense, profoundly appealing way. Strether describes her as a person who "won't be touched"; when he imagines her his eyes "might have been fixing some particularly large iceberg in a cool blue northern sea"; and, as we have seen, he refers to her, in her "tightly packed" fullness, as a "block." Her emotional coldness is seen by him, in these images, as an aspect of her larger impassivity, her resistance to any modification by worldly circumstance. This is why her being all "fine cold thought" "falls in" so well with her resistance to surprises. Solid and purely active as she is (essentially all *pressure* without response), life cannot leave a mark on her. It is not *permitted* to enter in, or to pull anything out. She is, Strether muses, the sort of meal that can be "serve cold" (represented by an ambassador) "without its really losing anything" of its essential flavor—so little does its character consist in responsiveness to what is at hand.

This connection between absence of emotion and absence of passivity is made long before on behalf of Woollett as a whole, when Strether tells Maria Gostrey, "Woollett isn't sure it ought to enjoy. If it were, it would." The first half of this remark is frequently quoted by critics; the second is, I think, even more significant. For it informs us that Woollett conceives of everything valuable in life as activity that can be morally willed. If it *were* sure that enjoyment was its duty, it would set itself to do that duty, it would simply will itself to enjoy. The oddness of this idea reminds us that some of the valuable things in life have more to do with passivity and responsiveness than with active willing; and their connection with "ought" is therefore to be viewed with deep suspicion.

—Martha C. Nussbaum, *Love's Knowledge: Essays on Philosophy and Literature* (NY: Oxford University Press, 1990): pp. 176–177.

Plot Summary of
The Golden Bowl

'Then it all depends on the bowl? I mean your future does? For that's what it comes to, I judge.'

> Bedizened and jewelled, in her rustling finery, she paid, with humility of attitude, this prompt tribute to order— only to find however that she could carry but two of the fragments at once. . . . With this she returned to the mantel-shelf, placing it with deliberation in the centre and then for a minute occupying herself as with the attempt to fit the other morsels together. The split determined by the latent crack was so sharp and so neat that if there had been anything to hold them the bowl might still quite beautifully, a few steps away, have passed for uninjured. As there was however nothing to hold them but Maggie's hands . . . she could only lay the almost equal parts of the vessel carefully besides their pedestal and leave them thus before her husband's eyes.

James takes care to be extremely clear about the relationship between the two couples and the flawed golden bowl, which, in spite of this title by which it is immediately and universally referred by the triangular relations, is not actually gold at all but crystal instead. Like the bowl, which is only called 'golden,' the marriages between Maggie and Amerigo, Adam and Charlotte are in many ways merely the appearance of the union and called so for the conventional appropriateness of the term. In fact, the author is amused to refer to Maggie and her father as 'married' before their respective marriages, and it is only because they are actually father and daughter that the two separate into different households with their chosen *sposi*.

Thus it is a uniquely sad state of affairs that for the sake of appearances and social expectation, Maggie and her father separate, just as Amerigo and Charlotte chose to end their affair on the technicality of their mutual poverty. The four, then, fit together like pieces of a jigsaw puzzle—Amerigo matches his royal lineage to Maggie's wealth, and Adam all too clearly recognizes that any collector of rare and beautiful art should be proud to add Charlotte to his collection. Yet the problem of these matches is that the pieces of the puzzle each have more than one side to join with another, and some of these junctures must remain concealed. The network of overt and covert relations among the four, with the frequent addition of Fanny Assingham, is an extremely complex and fragile balance that is made even more precarious by the carefully selective silences of the parties involved.

The golden bowl is the vessel that contains the narrative of the guilty parties. On the eve of Amerigo's marriage to Maggie, Charlotte solicits her former lover for one final private meeting, ostensibly for the purpose of searching for a wedding gift for the bride. It is on this venture that Charlotte discovers the ornament, which she desires to buy but cannot because it is beyond her means. She buys nothing, Amerigo marries the American heiress, and the order of their lives seems settled. For Adam Verver, however, equilibrium has not yet been achieved. He worries that his daughter is concerned over his welfare in his empty house after her marriage and decides that he must also marry in order to set her mind at rest. After consulting Maggie in their customary almost-telepathic manner of communication, Adam settles that Charlotte will prove extremely fit for the position. Again, order seems to have descended over the two households, but again, this structure is flawed. Comforted by having fulfilled their respective duties of marriage, father and daughter recommence their long hours of fellowship together, becoming even more encouraged to indulge themselves when they see how extraordinarily well their spouses get along even in their absence.

Amerigo and Charlotte's affair becomes an instance of hiding in plain sight, but Maggie finally shows that the two sophisticates have sorely mistaken her meekness as mental inferiority. The Princess first confronts Fanny Assingham with her suspicions, only to have the older woman lie baldly to save her friends on both sides. Even when confronted with the inevitability of the golden bowl, Fanny will not submit to the ugly truth, and demonstrates to her friend her determination to keep peace among the two households by smashing the crystal piece on the ground. Yet it appears that the golden bowl is more incriminating in its shattered state, for it breaks into three distinct pieces, which could be arranged such that it would appear whole from a distance. Having demonstrated this evidence of their marital failures before her husband, who respects both her heroic silence and the generosity of her forgiveness, Maggie is now completely in control, and she becomes the engineer of their mutual resolution.

The conversation between Maggie and her father that results in his decision to remove himself and his wife to America is an exquisite choreography of minute exchanges between the two speakers who, even in the most delicate improvisations, turn out a masterpiece of communication. Adam understands that he is expected to understand Maggie's fiction as necessary to correctly re-order their lives, and he accepts her claims of her own selfishness as reason enough to place the Atlantic between them. Maggie is similarly magnificent in her maneuvering of Charlotte, allowing her stepmother to successfully accuse her of attempting to create trouble in her father's marriage, in order that the older woman may depart to America with an idea of her own dignity. At the last, Maggie asserts her own destiny over that of the golden bowl, and the sacrifices of her own dignity are merely steps to her ultimate victory. Thus, Fanny Assingham misfires when she accuses Amerigo as a Machiavelli, for it is much more so the case that his wife holds the end in ultimate scope. ❁

List of Characters in
The Golden Bowl

Adam Verver: An American multimillionaire with a passion for collecting *objets d'art*. His first passion, however, is for his daughter, Maggie, and he marries her to the Prince with his full blessings. James consistently emphasizes Adam's youthfulness, which is a source of comfort to Maggie and a convenience in his marriage to Charlotte, who is only three years older than his daughter. Adam has developed a charming stoicism in defense of both himself and his beloved daughter such that he appears perpetually content.

Maggie Verver: Made a Princess by her marriage to Amerigo, Maggie, in many ways, does not appear to have the proper grand scope of royalty. However, her inward depth is hidden from most everyone, who easily underestimate her mental and spiritual capacities. Her love for her father and for her husband are both and distinctly sublime, and at last, she sacrifices the former for the sake of the latter. With what seems like inhuman patience and fortitude, Maggie noiselessly returns the two households to their appropriate order, and the result is that all parties involved return to their places with their respective self-regards as intact as possible.

The Prince, Amerigo: A penniless but authentic Italian prince, he is a social credit to the Ververs. Although he genuinely loves Maggie, his marriage to her is primarily that of convenience, because he remains in love with his mistress, Charlotte. However, the Prince fully realizes his economic position and ultimately shifts his loyalty to Maggie after she reveals her knowledge of her husband's affair with her stepmother.

Charlotte Stant: Maggie's friend from their earlier years in school. She and Amerigo were once lovers, who separated because both were too poor to support each other. Charlotte is 'wonderful'—sophisticated, accomplished and adventurous. She is not a 'fortune-hunter,' in the normal sense of the term, yet her marriage to Adam Verver is fortunate in that it allows her to quite comfortably continue her affair with Amerigo. When she is discovered by Maggie, Charlotte becomes utterly alienated—from her lover and her friends—and is forced to cross the ocean to America with her senior husband to maintain her personal dignity.

Fanny Assingham: She is both Amerigo's and Maggie's confidante who is guilty of having arranged their marriage despite the fact that she was aware of the Prince's feelings for another woman. When finally confronted by Maggie regarding her suspicions about Amerigo and Charlotte, Fanny lies to her friend in order to preserve the semblance of order.

Colonel Assingham: Fanny's husband. He is the characteristically detached observer in this novel whose narrative function is to listen to his meddlesome and talkative wife. As the intrigues deepen, however, even the Colonel betrays occasional interest. In fact, the Colonel is rather largely amused by the antics of the Ververs and their respective *sposi.* ❁

Critical Views on
The Golden Bowl

[Stephen Spender (1909–1995), poet and critic, was one of
James's earliest critics. He was famous for his intimacy with
the literary giants of his age, including Virginia Woolf,
W. H. Auden, and T. S. Eliot. His many poetic works include
Poems from Spain, Ruins and Visions, The Generous Days. He
was Professor of English at University College, London, and
was knighted in 1983. In this excerpt, Spender notes the
structural symmetry of *The Golden Bowl* and discusses its
literary relationship to modern poetry.]

The Golden Bowl is extremely simplified, because there are only four
main characters and two subsidiary choric figures, and no one else is
of the slightest importance. The key to the situation is the fact that
there are, in effect, before the action begins, two original groupings.
Maggie is the companion of her father, Mr. Verver, and they live
together in their relationship always gaily referred to as their marriage. Meanwhile, unknown to them, their two future *sposi*—as they
are always called—Amerigo, the prince, and Charlotte, an adventurous, moneyless, "wonderful" friend of Maggie, are having their
little affair. The leading choric character, Mrs. Assingham, now
steps in and breaks up the grouping from *AB, CD*—Maggie, Mr.
Verver: the prince, Charlotte; into *AC, BD*. The prince marries
Maggie. Maggie is now deeply conscious of the loneliness of her
father, and her father is also conscious that her concern for him may
not be best for her marriage. Meanwhile, Charlotte returns from
America, and, just before the wedding, she walks through Mayfair
with the prince, where, in a curio shop, they look at the golden bowl
with a flaw in it, which they discuss, but decide not to buy, for
Maggie's wedding present. After the marriage, Charlotte stays with
the Ververs, and then Mr. Verver takes her to Brighton, and proposes
to her. They marry, and soon after the marriage, the prince and
Charlotte start living together. Thus, after a transition, in which the
figures are *AC, BD,* we return to the original order *AB, CD*. The dramatic climax of the book is Maggie's passionate fight to restore the

order of the marriages, which she at last succeeds in doing. Thus the book falls into this sort of pattern:—

Spectators	AB	CD	
	The Golden Bowl		
The Colonel and Fanny	AC	BD	The Colonel and Fanny
Assingham	AB	CD	Assingham
	The Golden Bowl		
	AC	BD	

This symmetry symbolizes the social order.

The golden bowl with its flaw represents, of course, the flaw in the order of their lives. ⟨. . .⟩

⟨. . .⟩ The struggle of the Ververs is a struggle to make the picture fit the frame; they are constantly struggling to make their lives worthy of their dead surroundings. ⟨. . .⟩

⟨. . .⟩ It is emphasized throughout the book that everything about them is, by mere contrast with their huge setting, very small. Their virtues are a human understanding which does not extend beyond the individuals immediately around them, and immense personal tenderness, and a love which hardly reaches further than each other and the pair whom they marry. The word "small" is constantly associated with Maggie, and it is she who in one of her moments of greatest exaltation realizes that her father was "simply a great and deep and high little man, and that to love him with tenderness was not to be distinguished, a whit, from loving him with pride." One remembers him always, with his dim smile, his quiet, very youthful manner, in the unassuming little scene; gazing at a "piece" in his collection, or wandering vaguely about his garden. On the other hand, everything about Charlotte and the prince is on the grand scale. ⟨. . .⟩

Throughout *The Golden Bowl* the descriptive passages deliberately suggest vast spaces opening out into mystery and vagueness. ⟨. . .⟩

It is from this deliberately conjured atmosphere that there arise, as from the depths, the dream images of the unconscious. Too often these images, not being ordered by metric, almost overwhelm the reader, swamping all other associations, and making him forget the story. ⟨. . .⟩

It is the feeling of horror, of foreboding before some calamity, that never fails, and that sometimes produces a poetry so pure and so dreadfully true of our whole situation, that it reaches far beyond the "small despair" of the Ververs. ⟨. . .⟩

It is such passages in James, which in their use of imagery derived from everyday life, predict the best in modern poetry. But the feeling of a horror that is entirely modern, is emphasized even more strongly, in the passages which describe the mental suffering of Maggie. ⟨. . .⟩

⟨. . .⟩ When one considers these examples, one begins to feel certain that beneath the stylistic surface, the portentous snobbery, the golden display of James's work, there lurk forms of violence and chaos. His technical mastery has the perfection of frightful balance and frightful tension: beneath the stretched-out compositions there are abysses of despair and disbelief: *Ulysses* and *The Waste Land.*

—Stephen Spender, *The Destructive Element: A Study of Modern Writers and Beliefs* (London: J. Cape, 1935): pp. 320–326.

AUSTIN WARREN ON SYMBOLIC IMAGERY

[Austin Warren (1877–1963), biographer of the elder James, was Professor Emeritus of English at the University of Michigan. Among his many books are *Alexander Pope as Critic and Humanist, Connections,* and *Theory of Literature.* In this selection, Warren discusses the metaphorical and art-based imagery, especially regarding Maggie, in *The Golden Bowl.*]

Recollected images become metaphors. For years James had traveled diligently in France and Italy, written conscientious commentaries on cathedrals, châteaux, and galleries. Now people remind him of art, become indeed works of art. His heroines, almost without exception, are thus translated. The auburn-haired Milly Theale is a Bronzino; Aurora Coyne becomes "an Italian princess of the *cinque cento:* Titian or the grand Veronese might . . . have signed her image."

Nan, the modernist and un-British daughter of *The Sense of the Past,* recalls "some mothering Virgin by Van Eyck or Memling." For Maggie there is evoked some slim draped statue from the Vatican, "the smoothed elegant nameless head, the impersonal flit of a creature lost in an alien age." Mme de Vionnet's head could be found on "an old precious medal, some silver coin of the Renaissance," while her daughter is a "faint pastel in an oval frame . . . the portrait of an old-time princess." Some embarrassment prevents similar translation of the heroes into paintings or statues; but the Prince (who is bought, after all, as a work of art and appraised by his father-in-law with the same taste which appraises a Luini) can scarcely be described except out of art history: by way of representing the superior utility and weight of the male, James renders him in architecture. His eyes, for example, prompt the *concetto* of their being "the high windows of a Roman palace, of an historic front by one of the great old designers, thrown open on a feast day to the golden air." And his union to the Ververs, the new "relation" which it establishes, suggests to Adam Verver that "their decent little old-time union, Maggie's and his own, had resembled a good deal some pleasant public square, in the heart of an old city, into which a great Palladian church, say—something with a grand architectural front—had suddenly been dropped." ⟨. . .⟩

The chief occasions for "imaging" are perceptions of persons and personal relations. In *The Bowl* and the unfinished novels, the characters are not visualized analytically but felt for us, rendered in terms of the total impression they make. ⟨. . .⟩

⟨. . .⟩ Throughout most of her half of *The Golden Bowl,* Maggie is the "overworked little trapezist girl." The novel rehearses her progress from being a child to being the lady in spangled skirts who can keep her balance while she capers on the back of a horse.

There are other fresh aspects of Maggie to be celebrated—for one, her resourceful Americanism—in contrast to her husband's ancient, aristocratic lineage. By virtue of this difference, Maggie must be expected to do most of the "adjustment": she must act like a "settler or trader in a new country; in the likeness even of some Indian squaw with a papoose on her back and barbarous bead work to sell." But without question there are governing images. As Maggie is the trapezist, so Charlotte, through the corresponding second half of *The Bowl,* is some wild creature, tormented by the gadfly; she is a caged creature which, bending the gilt bars, has escaped to roam; she wears "a long silken halter looped round her beautiful neck."

In the later novels the chief thing, after all, is the structure. The characters exist in relations, and we are unbidden to information about them irrelevant to the fable and the relations. A character might almost be defined as the locus at which a given number of relations join. ⟨...⟩

The second half of *The Golden Bowl*, supreme among the later novels for the density and richness of its symbolism, is dominated by Maggie's sense of the relations in which she stands, of which the most stable is with her father, the most precarious and menacing that with her rival, the Dark Lady.

The "imagings"—fear-images, many of them—which crowd the later chapters arise from Maggie's inability to talk out her apprehensions except, and scantily, to Mrs. Assingham. Her relations to her father, the Prince, and Charlotte cannot, by the very nature of her problem and her project, be socially articulated; she must fight soundlessly and in the dark. ⟨...⟩

In spite of the predominance of myth over dialectic in the novel, especially its second half, *The Bowl* does not represent James's escape into a defeatist Unconscious, the collapse of his system of values. Unlike many of his protagonists, Maggie is concerned not only to understand her situation but to will, savingly, and to act, successfully. Her dreams are, ultimately, those not of a patient but of a victor.

—Austin Warren, Rage for Order (Michigan: University of Michigan Press, 1959): pp. 142–161.

Adeline Tintner on the Museum World

[Adeline Tintner is the author of numerous works on Edith Wharton and Henry James, including *Cosmopolitan World of Henry James, Museum World of Henry James,* and *Edith Wharton: Essays on Intertextuality.* She is an independent scholar living in New York City. This excerpt notes how the role of Adam Verver as art collector arranges the other characters in the novel as part of his collection as well.]

If Milly, "the heiress of all the ages," could possess Europe only through its art, its life passing her by, Adam Verver of *The Golden Bowl* finally possesses Europe in its material form as art and its spiritual form as personality. The price he must pay is the sacrifice of his innocence, his Americanism. ("American life is, on the whole, as I make no doubt whatever, more innocent than that of any other country," James had written in 1886.) He must submit to experience. There are two main myths which can be extracted from what James in his preface calls "the gathered cluster of all the *kinds* of interest." One, the myth of the discovery by the new world (innocence) and the old world (experience) of each other, operates only in key metaphors in the consciousness of the characters. Adam, the new world, compares himself to the discoverer Cortez rifling "the Golden Isles," even subconsciously using the legend of Cortez' burning of his ships, when he proposes to Charlotte. Amerigo, the Prince, in "discovering the Americans," enters his "port of the Golden Isles" in the image of Vespucci, his ancestor. Subsidiary images reinforce this opposition of innocence to experience: Adam is the "natural fowl running round the basse-cour"; Amerigo is "cooked down as a crème de volaille"; Adam is the first man living the life of innocence and ignorance in the "state before the Fall." The Prince is "steeped" in history "as in some chemical bath." The opposition in this basic myth provides the necessary motivation for the overt myth, that of the American's view of Europe's civilization, both art and life, as objects for a collection. For the Cortez complex in Adam takes the form of art patron with such intensity that the Prince becomes a crystal; Charlotte, Oriental tiles; and even his daughter, some "draped antique of Vatican or Capitoline halls." Parallel to this effect the Prince's Vespucci complex determines the elements of his experience as colored by what he receives as his end of the bargain in presenting himself as a morceau de musée—money! Charlotte for him is "some long, loose purse well filled with gold pieces," her words of assignation "the chink . . . of gold in his ear," their day together "some great gold cup." These two myths are joined on the level of action by an object of art itself, a golden bowl, which, first a symbol of Amerigo's and Charlotte's adultery, becomes a symbol of the Ververs' deformed attitude to their precious people. For when people are treated like works of art, certain human needs are ignored which will eventually assert themselves and turn the tables on those who possess them. Thus Amerigo and Charlotte, in their private intrigue, actually "fixed" Maggie and Adam. The bowl, therefore, as a real symbol of an unnatural point of view, is broken by Mrs. Assingham, the Greek chorus who interprets the real meaning of experience to both the characters of the drama and to the reader. When Maggie and Adam at the end of the novel review their possessions, they know that to deserve them they must accept all of the experience which they contain, its good and evil. The possession of rare objects is only assured when their complex human values are understood. The "mystic meaning proper to themselves" of the spoils of Europe is that they incorporate all the values of experience, and must be understood through experience itself.

—Adeline Tintner, "The Museum World," (originally entitled "The Spoils of Henry James") *PMLA* 61 (1946): pp. 239–251.

FREDERICK C. CREWS ON *THE GOLDEN BOWL*

[Frederick C. Crews is Professor Emeritus of English at the University of California, Berkeley. His work includes *The Sins of the Fathers: Hawthorne's Psychological Themes, The Pooh Perplex: A Freshman Casebook, Out of My System: Psychoanalysis, Ideology, and Critical Method,* and *The Critics Bear It Away: American Fiction and the Academy.* This selection highlights the power struggle between the four main characters in *The Golden Bowl.*]

The subject of the novel, in my opinion, is power. What is its nature? Who possesses it? What are its moral implications? These, I think, are the questions posed with the deepest urgency. Each of the characters is seeking control over the others, or resisting their control, or deliberately acquiescing in it. Each has the matter of social dominance in the front of his consciousness. The four main characters represent four distinct kinds of power, and the motion of the book is a gradual shift in emphasis from the power of one character to that of another. We come to recognize the power of each, but realize with every change of focus that the person now under observation is stronger than his predecessor. At the end of the novel we have made out fairly well who is the most powerful character and why. The final and greatest exercise of power dissolves the situation which called for a test in the first place. ⟨. . .⟩

Power, then, is seen to consist in several virtues, both Christian and Machiavellian, but above all in the virtue of not letting one's antagonists know what is on one's mind. Maggie is superior to both Charlotte and Amerigo in this respect. But if inscrutability is the key to power, no one can deny that Adam Verver holds that key. This is the truth that becomes increasingly plain as the novel unfolds, until at the finish everyone has discovered for himself that Adam is supreme. He not only is the chief source of their own power, but has a great amount of it reserved to himself—more than anyone is capable of guessing. His success depends on just this ability to mask his strength. As he reflects, "Everyone has need of one's power, whereas one's own need, at the best, would have seemed to be but some trick for not communicating it." Adam succeeds, where even Maggie fails, in remaining altogether out of the foreground. He paces quietly across "the further end of any watched perspective," making no demands, asking no questions, but merely reminding the others of his presence. His raw power—that is to say, the other characters' estimation of his power—is sufficiently eloquent in itself.

—Frederick C. Crews, *The Tragedy of Manners: Moral Drama in the Later Novels of Henry James* (New Haven, CT: Yale University Press, 1957): pp. 85–89.

JOHN BAYLEY ON LOVE AND KNOWLEDGE IN THE NOVEL

[John Bayley is Warton Professor of English at Oxford University. Among his many books are *The Romantic Survival: A Study in Poetic Evolution, The Characters of Love: A Study in the Literature of Personality, Tolstoy and the Novel, Pushkin: A Comparative Commentary,* and *Essays on Hardy.*

In this excerpt, Bayley discusses the poignancy of silence in the relationship between knowledge, love, and power in *The Golden Bowl*.]

The punishment of the knowers, as Fanny points out, including herself in the category, is this terrible indifference to knowledge which confounds and controls them, holding them in a state of uneasy speculation. ⟨. . .⟩

In *The Golden Bowl* we certainly feel that the sharp taste of uncertainty has been added to our quickened sense of life, and it is a sense of life which comes precisely from the absence of openness and revelation. ⟨. . .⟩

The high priest of soundlessness is of course Adam Verver, and he, even more than Maggie, embodies the idea that suffocating the facts instead of liberating them is society's sagest moral expedient. Before concluding, we should therefore perhaps examine him rather more closely. James in his *Notebooks* refers to him as 'a product', a product somehow of America, even though a very exceptional, remarkable, and striking one. He is fabulously rich, of course, and is making a collection of beautiful things which will eventually form a museum in his home town. His wealth is partly inherited but he has also increased it himself, presumably setting his teeth and somehow forcing himself through what James calls the 'livid vulgarity of getting in, or getting out, first'. He is a widower, and we are told that he and his first wife 'had loved each other so that his intelligence, on the higher line, had temporarily paid for it'. We can take it for granted that the characters in James's novels will be vividly present to us in their physical selves, and Verver is no exception, he appears before us with his mild eye and his cigar, his waistcoat, his little strolls, and his air at the head of his dinner-table of 'an innocent little boy'. Yet he remains a visionary figure, eloquent of the difference between the American millionaire as he was and as James would have liked him to be. So much the worse for the American millionaire, James might retort, as he retorted of the presumed non-existence of his American poet, Jeffrey Aspern, and the 'supersubtle' authors in *The Figure in the Carpet*. But in the case of Verver this appeal to the artist's freedom in creation will perhaps not quite do. For one thing American millionaire collectors *did* very much exist, men who indeed saw 'acquisition of one sort as a perfect preliminary to acquisition of another', but upon whom the metaphor bestowed on Verver's career—'the years of darkness had been needed to render possible the years of light'—would be grotesquely lost. So we may feel that Verver should be the Aristotelian 'real because impossible' character, but succeeds only in being an unreal because improbable one. And it is this lack of coherence between Verver as a visionary figure and as a convincing personality that makes him strike us as a monster.

—John Bayley, *The Characters of Love: A Study in the Literature of Personality* (NY: Basic Books, 1960): pp. 205–262.

Oscar Cargill on *The Golden Bowl*

[Oscar Cargill is the head of the English Department at New York University. He has written a wide range of articles on contemporary literature, including *Thomas Wolfe at Washington Square* and *Intellectual America*. He is editor of anthologies from the writings of Henry James, Walt Whitman, Henry David Thoreau, and of *American Literature: A Period Anthology*. In this selection, Cargill focuses on James's formal decision of dividing the novel into two opposite perspectives, that of the Prince and the Princess. Cargill also notes the narrative function of the Assinghams.]

The concentration of James's analysis on his principals though the mind of the Prince chiefly in the first book and that of the Princess almost exclusively in the second results in a work which is perhaps the most nearly ultimate and finest expression of the Turgenev method, in which, as we have seen, we know only what we discern from the action and speech of the characters, whose revelation is our chief concern, since their capacities or limitations determine the outcome of the story. It would seem, without reflection, that James had done some violence to that method by adopting first one interior point of view and then another, but actually the omniscience of each principal, when the point of view is his or hers, is peculiarly limited by ignorance of the motives of the persons who are, in turn, of chief concern. Thus the Prince knows less than we about his wife and father-in-law in the first book and Maggie is in ignorance of the true feelings of her husband in the second, our view of his mental processes being cut off just at the moment when they would reveal too much to us. In each book surmised intent is developed into real intent in characters closely related to the principals: the Prince surmises why Charlotte has returned to London and his surmise is validated; the Princess assumes that her father's loyalty is not divided to her disadvantage and so it proves, though Charlotte causes her one deeply shaken moment before their relationship is resolved. There is the most ingenious and cunning balancing of "knowns" and "unknowns" in an almost mathematical sense as the narrative progresses, giving *The Golden Bowl* the character of a play by Racine, as Francis Fergusson has acutely observed, for "a comedy of manners" is not an adequate descriptive phase, as a comparison with the contemporaneous *Lady Windemere's Fan* or *Michael and His Lost Angel* would reveal. It is too finely affirmative for the technical phrase to have more than the most hollow meaning.

Yet, in choosing Colonel Assingham and Fanny as commentators on the principals, James certainly is exploiting a device more common to the plays of Wilde, Jones, and Pinero than to Greek tragedy, as has sometimes been suggested. Mrs. Wharton, who is among those to make such a suggestion, is the harshest critic of the device:

> In *The Golden Bowl,* still unsatisfied, still in pursuit of an impossible perfection, he felt he must introduce a sort of *co-ordinating consciousness,* detached from but including, the characters principally concerned. The same attempt to wrest dramatic forms to the uses of the novel that caused *The Awkward Age* to be written in dialogue seems to have suggested the creation of Colonel and Mrs. Assingham as a sort of Greek chorus to the tragedy of *The Golden Bowl.* This insufferable and incredible couple spend their days in espionage and delation, and their evenings in exchanging the reports of their eavesdropping with a minuteness and precision worthy of Scotland Yard. The utter improbability of such conduct on the part of a dull-witted and frivolous couple in the rush of London society shows the author created them for the sole purpose of revealing details which he could not otherwise communicate.

This is very rough treatment, coming as it does from the novelist who had shown her own Lily Bart partially destroyed by gossip; further, it is mistaken. While the Assinghams do supply some information we do not otherwise possess, it is not true we could not possess it in a different manner had James so chosen (he was never lacking means); but that is not their sole function. Bob Assingham and his wife are "worriers" and they are sufficiently involved in the resolution of the four-sided triangle so that their worry is realistic and plausible. Their anxiety, particularly Fanny's, adds to the tension of the book and helps us more keenly to feel Maggie Verver's. ⟨. . .⟩ The Assinghams, a technically interesting device, really add immeasurably to the drama of *The Golden Bowl*. They preserve the dignity of the principals by accepting the burden of the mundane in what is, for all the exquisiteness of Charlotte Stant and the Prince, an exceptionally sordid relationship.

—Oscar Cargill, *The Novels of Henry James* (NY: Macmillan Company, 1961): pp. 422–424.

Works by
Henry James

Pyramus and Thisbe. 1869.

Still Waters. 1871.

Watch and Ward. 1871.

A Change of Heart. 1872.

A Passionate Pilgrim and Other Tales. 1875.

Transatlantic Sketches. 1875.

Roderick Hudson. 1875.

The American. 1877.

French Poets and Novelists. 1878.

The Europeans. 1878.

Daisy Miller. 1878.

An International Episode. 1879.

The Madonna of the Future and Other Tales. 1879.

Hawthorne. 1879.

The Diary of a Man of Fifty; A Bundle of Letters. 1880.

Confidence. 1880.

Washington Square. 1880.

The Portrait of a Lady. 1881.

The Siege of London; The Pension Beaurepas; The Point of View. 1883.

Portraits of Places. 1883.

Tales of Three Cities. 1884.

The Art of Fiction (with W. Besant). 1885.

The Author of Beltraffio. 1885.

A Little Tour in France. 1885.

Stories Revived. 1885.

The Bostonians. 1886.

The Princess Casamassima. 1886.

Partial Portraits. 1888.

The Aspern Papers; Louisa Pallant; The Modern Warning. 1888.

The Reverberator. 1888.

A London Life; The Patagonia; The Liar; Mrs. Temperley. 1889.

The Tragic Muse. 1890.

The Lesson of the Master; The Marriages. The Wheel of Time. 1892.

The Private Life. 1893.

Essays in London and Elsewhere. 1893.

The Real Thing. 1893.

The Album. 1894.

Theatricals: Two Comedies—Tenants; Disengaged. 1894.

The Reprobate. 1894.

Theatricals, Second Series. 1895.

Terminations; The Death of the Lion. 1895.

Embarrassments. 1896.

The Other House. 1896.

The Spoils of Poynton. 1897.

What Maisie Knew. 1897.

The Two Magics; The Turn of the Screw; Covering End. 1898.

In the Cage. 1898.

The Awkward Age. 1899.

The Soft Side. 1900.

The Sacred Fount. 1901.

The Wings of the Dove. 1902.

William Wetmore Story and His Friends. 1903.

The Better Sort. 1903.

The Ambassadors. 1903.

The Golden Bowl. 1904.

The Question of Our Speech; The Lesson of Balzac. 1905.

English Hours. 1905.

The American Scene. 1907.

The Novels and Tales of Henry James
(known as the New York Edition). 1907–1917.

Views and Reviews. 1908.

Julia Bride. 1909.

Italian Hours. 1909.

The Finer Grain. 1909.

The Outcry. 1911.

A Small Boy and Others. 1913.

Notes of a Son and Brother. 1914.

Notes on Novelists. 1914.

The Question of Mind. 1915.

Letters from America. 1916.

The Ivory Tower. 1917.

The Middle Years. 1917.

The Sense of the Past. 1917.

Within the Rim and Other Essays, 1914–1915. 1918.

Gabrieele de Bergerac. 1918.

Travelling Companions. 1919.

Monologue Written for Ruth Draper. 1922.

The Notebooks of Henry James. 1947.

The American (play). 1949.

The High Bid. 1949.

Guy Domville. 1949.

The Other House (play). 1949.

The Outcry (play). 1949.

*Rough Statement for Three Acts Founded on the
Chaperon* (play). 1949.

The Saloon (play). 1949.

Summersoft (play). 1949.

The Ghostly Tales of Henry James. 1949.

Eight Uncollected Tales. 1950.

The American Essay. 1956.

The Future of the Novel. 1956.

Parisian Sketches. 1957.

Literary Reviews and Essays on American,
  English, and French Literature. 1957.

The Art of Travel. 1958.

French Writers and American Women. 1960.

The Complete Tales of Henry James (12 volumes). 1962–1964.

Selected Literary Criticism. 1963.

Letters of Henry James (4 volumes). 1974–1984.

Literary Criticism. 1984.

The Art of Criticism. 1986.

The Critical Muse. 1987.

Collected Travel Writing. 1993.

Traveling in Italy with Henry James. 1994.

Works about
Henry James

Armstrong, Paul B. *The Phenomenology of Henry James.* Chapel Hill, NC: University of North Carolina Press, 1983.

Auchard, John. *Silence in Henry James: The Heritage of Symbolism and Decadence.* University Park: Pennsylvania State University Press, 1986.

Auchincloss, Louis. *Reading Henry James.* Minneapolis: University of Minnesota Press, 1975.

Beach, Joseph Warren. *The Method of Henry James.* New Haven, CT: Yale University Press, 1918.

Bell, Millicent. *Meaning in Henry James.* Cambridge, MA: Harvard University Press, 1991.

Blair, Sara. *Henry James and the Writing of Race and Nation.* Cambridge, England: Cambridge University Press, 1996.

Bloom, Harold, ed. *Henry James.* New York: Chelsea House Publishers, 1987.

———. *Henry James' The Ambassadors.* New York: Chelsea House Publishers, 1988.

———. *Henry James' The Portrait of a Lady.* New York: Chelsea House Publishers, 1987.

Booth, Wayne C. *The Rhetoric of Fiction.* Chicago: University of Chicago Press, 1961.

Bradbury, Nicola. *An Annotated Critical Bibliography of Henry James.* Brighton, Sussex: Harvester Press, 1987.

Brodhead, Richard H. *The School of Hawthorne.* New York: Oxford University Press, 1986.

Brooks, Peter. *The Melodramatic Imagination: Balzac, Henry James, Melodrama, and the Mode of Excess.* New Haven, CT: Yale University Press, 1976.

Brooks, V. W. *Pilgrimage of Henry James.* New York: E. P. Dutton & Company, 1925.

Buitenhuis, Peter. *The Grasping Imagination: The American Writings of Henry James.* Toronto: University of Toronto Press, 1970.

Cameron, Sharon. *Thinking in Henry James.* Chicago: University of Chicago, 1989.

Clarke, Graham, ed. *Henry James: Critical Assessments.* East Sussex: Helm Information Ltd., 1991.

Crews, Frederick C. *The Tragedy of Manners: Moral Drama in the Later Novels of Henry James.* New Haven, CT: Yale University Press, 1957.

Dupee, F. W. *Henry James.* New York: William Sloane Associates, 1951.

———— ed. *The Question of Henry James: A Collection of Critical Essays.* New York: H. Holt and Company, 1945.

Edel, Leon. *Henry James* (5 volumes). Philadelphia: Lippincott, 1953–1972.

————. *Henry James: A Collection of Critical Essays.* Englewood Cliffs, NJ: Prentice-Hall, 1963.

————. *A Bibliography of Henry James.* London: R. Hart-Davis, 1957.

Fogel, Daniel Mark. *Henry James and the Structure of the Romantic Imagination.* Baton Rouge: Louisiana State University Press, 1981.

————. *A Companion to Henry James Studies.* Westport, CT: Greenwood Press, 1993.

Freedman, Jonathan. *Professions of Taste: Henry James, British Aestheticism and Commodity Culture.* Stanford, CA: Stanford University Press, 1990.

Funston, J. E. *Henry James: A Reference Guide, 1975–1987.* Boston: G. K. Hall & Co., 1991.

Gard, Roger, ed. *Henry James: The Critical Heritage.* London, England: Routledge & K. Paul, 1968.

Goode, John, ed. *The Air of Reality: New Essays on Henry James.* London: Methuen, 1972.

Hardy, Barbara. *Henry James: The Later Writing.* Plymouth, UK: Northcote House Publishers Ltd., 1996.

Holland, L. *The Expense of Vision: Essays on the Craft of Henry James.* Princeton, NJ: Princeton University Press, 1964.

Howe, Irving. *Politics and the Novel.* New York: Horizon Press, 1957.

Jameson, Fredric. *Marxism and Form: Twentieth-Century Dialectical Theories of Literature.* Princeton, NJ: Princeton University Press, 1971.

Jones, Granville H. *Henry James' Psychology of Experience: Innocence, Responsibility, and Renunciation in the Fiction of Henry James.* Netherlands: Mouton & Co. N.V., Publishers, 1975.

Kaston, Carren. *Imagination and Desire in the Novels of Henry James.* New Brunswick, NJ: Rutgers University Press, 1984.

Kazin, Alfred. *On Native Grounds: An Interpretation of Modern American Prose Literature.* New York: Harcourt, Brace & World, 1942.

Krook, Dorothea. *The Ordeal of Consciousness in Henry James.* Cambridge, England: Cambridge University Press, 1962.

Leavis, F.R. *The Great Tradition.* Garden City, New York: Doubleday, 1954.

Lebowitz, Naomi. *Discussions of Henry James.* UK.: Heath, 1962.

Lee, Brian. *The Novels of Henry James: A Study of Culture and Consciousness.* London: Edward Arnold, 1978.

Leeming, Glenda. *Who's Who in Henry James.* New York: Taplinger Pub. Co., 1976.

Lewis, Pericles. *Modernism, Nationalism, and the Novel.* New York: Cambridge University Press, 2000.

Lubbock, Percy. *The Craft of Fiction.* NY: Viking Press, 1957.

Matthiessen, F. O. *Henry James: The Major Phase.* New York: Oxford University Press, 1944.

Mackenzie, Manfred. *Communities of Honor and Love in Henry James.* Cambridge, MA: Harvard University Press, 1976.

McWhirter, David Bruce. *Desire and Love in Henry James: A Study of the Late Novels.* New York: Cambridge University Press, 1989.

Meissner, Collin. *Henry James and the Language of Experience.* Cambridge, England: Cambridge University Press, 1999.

Miller, J. Hillis. *The Ethics of Reading: Kant, de Man, Eliot, Trollope, James, and Benjamin.* New York: Columbia University Press, 1987.

Newton, Ruth & Naomi Lebowitz. *Dickens, Manzoni, Zola & James: The Impossible Romance.* Columbia: University of Missouri Press, 1990.

Nussbaum, Martha. *Love's Knowledge: Essays on Philosophy and Literature.* New York: Oxford University Press, 1990.

Pippin, Robert B. *Henry James and Modern Moral Life.* Cambridge: Cambridge University Press, 2000.

Poirier, Richard. *The Comic Sense of Henry James: A Study of the Early Novels.* NY: Oxford University Press, 1960.

Posnock, Ross. *The Trial of Curiosity: Henry James, William James, and the Challenge of Modernity.* NY: Oxford University Press, 1991.

Samuels, Charles Thomas. *The Ambiguity of Henry James.* Urbana: University of Illinois Press, 1971.

Sears, Sallie. *The Negative Imagination: Form and Perspective in the Novels of Henry James.* NY: Cornell University Press, 1968.

Segal, Ora. *The Lucid Reflector: The Observers in Henry James' Fiction.* New Haven, CT: Yale University Press, 1969.

Seltzer, Mark. *Henry James and the Art of Power.* Ithaca: Cornell University Press, 1984.

Sicker, Philip. *Love and the Quest for Identity in the Fiction of Henry James.* Princeton, NJ: Princeton University Press, 1980.

Spender, Stephen. *The Destructive Element: A Study of Modern Writers and Beliefs.* London, England: J. Cape, 1935.

Trilling, Lionel. *Liberal Imagination: Essays on Literature and Society.* NY: Viking Press, 1950.

Vann, J. Don. *Critics on Henry James.* Coral Gables, FL: University of Miami Press, 1972.

Walton, Priscilla L. *The Disruption of the Feminine in Henry James.* Toronto: University of Toronto Press, 1992.

Wegelin, Christof. *The Image of Europe in Henry James.* Dallas, TX: Southern Methodist University Press, 1958.

Weinstein, Philip M. *Henry James and the Requirements of the Imagination.* Cambridge, MA: Harvard University Press, 1971.

Yeazell, Ruth. *The Death and Letters of Alice James.* Berkeley, CA: University of California Press, 1981.

———. *Language and Knowledge in the Late Novels of Henry James.* Chicago: University of Chicago Press, 1976.

Zwerdling, Alex. *Improvised Europeans: American Literary Expatriates and the Seige of London.* NY: Basic Books, 1998.

Index of
Themes and Ideas

WINGS OF THE DOVE, THE, 14, 51–67; abstraction in, 58–59; animal imagery in, 53, 56–57, 60, 61, 64–65; central role of Densher in, 62–63; characters in, 54–55; Christian ethic in, 63; consciousness of Kate Croy *versus* Milly Theale in, 57, 60, 66–67; critical views on, 56–67; Kate Croy in, 51–52, 53, 56, 60, 61, 62, 63, 64, 66–67; Lionel Croy in, 51, 67; Merton Densher in, 51, 52, 53, 54, 56, 57, 59–63; Aunt Maud Lowder in, 51, 52, 53, 54–55, 56, 57, 60, 80; Lord Mark in, 52, 55, 63; metaphor and Milly Theale in, 53, 64–65; plot summary of, 51–53; repudiation and redemption in Densher in, 62–63; Sir Luke Strett in, 52, 55, 56; Susan Stringham in, 52, 53, 55, 62–63, 65; Milly Theale in, 52–53, 54, 56–57, 58–59, 60–61, 62, 63, 64–65, 66–67, 91, 94; Milly Theale's clothes in, 57, 65; Milly Theale's prototype in, 58–59